I

Look

LIKE ME

A Celebration of Self-Love

I
Look
LIKE ME

A Celebration of Self-Love

Paula K. Dieck

ISBN: 978-0-692-27111-7

First Printing: September, 2014

DEDICATION

This book is dedicated to my wonderful parents,
Del and Karalee Dieck, who gave me a loving home
and a fantastic life. They provided a solid foundation
and gave their full support through every step of my
journey.

I would also like to acknowledge my husband who
encouraged the writing of this book. Through tears and
laughter, he has always been there for me.

And to the countless number of people through the
years, who after hearing my story said,
"You should write a book about your life."

Thank you.

I love each and every one of you.

Preface

I Look Like Me is my story. It is an account of my life events and my feelings about them, having been adopted as an infant and raised with the knowledge that I was adopted.

I would like to preface this story by saying that I was raised in a very loving family - by wonderful parents who "chose" me. My adoptive parents are "salt of the earth" people and could not have provided a more loving home. I always felt and knew that their love for me was and continues to be genuine. I am eternally grateful for them.

Throughout the story I will refer to my adoptive parents as "my mom" and "my dad" or as "my parents."

I also want to acknowledge my birth mother. I can't possibly know or begin to understand what she went through as a young adult, becoming pregnant out of wedlock at a time when this was socially unacceptable and then ultimately giving me up for adoption. I can only imagine the fear, shame and pain she must have endured throughout the process.

This book is about my journey as an adopted child; the happiness I felt, as well as the emptiness. Ultimately, it is about discovery, personal growth, forgiveness, and eventually, coming to a place of self-love.

As a teenager and into my twenties, I thought that I was the only person in the world who felt the way I did. I had low self-esteem. I felt like I wasn't good enough, that I was different from everyone else, and I wondered what was wrong with me.

Later, I became aware of how prevalent adoption is and I began to understand that I wasn't the only one with those feelings. Through personal encounters with other adult adoptees and through the research I studied, I realized that many of us have had feelings of inadequacy - feelings that stem from a sense of abandonment.

Unfortunately, it is not just adoptees that experience these feelings. There are a multitude of situations and circumstances which can leave a child feeling abandoned. Some of them are divorce, single parent homes, families with workaholic parents who may not have time for their children, or parents who are unable to openly or effectively express their love for their children, to name just a few.

A sense of abandonment and the feelings associated with it can negatively impact one's entire life, especially if the person is not aware of the core issue.

Fortunately, there are ways to recognize and break the patterns and to heal those emotional wounds, which is why I chose to write this book.

My hope is that all who read this book will find within it at least one piece of information to assist them with their own journey.

Paula K. Dieck

CHAPTER ONE

It was still dark and cold outside at 5:15 am. The young woman had been in the delivery room for hours and was now finally resting after giving birth. She was alone, scared and exhausted when the nurse came to her and told her that she had a healthy baby girl. At that same moment, the baby was taken from the delivery room to the nursery, without having been seen or held by her mother.

The newborn lay in the nursery unaware of the reality and the magnitude of what had just happened. There had been no connection or bonding with the mother. The child was alone. That night had stolen a piece of the baby's soul, leaving a void which would affect her for the rest of her life.

That baby was me. I was born in April, 1966 in Milwaukee, Wisconsin, and was immediately placed in a foster home where I stayed for nine weeks. Obviously, I don't consciously remember anything about those first, formative weeks of my life, but I wasn't with my own family and it wasn't a permanent situation.

In August of that year, I was adopted into a wonderful family and was raised in a small town in central Wisconsin.

My parents already had two biological sons who were 6 and 4 years old. From what I understand, the deliveries were very hard on my adopted mother and the doctor had suggested that she not get pregnant again. I guess they wanted a girl, and they say that they had talked about adopting for a long time. That's when they adopted me and named me Paula.

From the first day they brought me home, my parents told me that I was adopted. Of course, I was an infant and had no clue of what was going on in the world around me. As I grew and became more aware, I realized what it meant to be adopted. My mom was not the person who had given birth to me, but I was part of the family via legal process.

My parents always said that I was extra special because they had "chosen" me. My dad didn't say I was "the apple of his eye," but that I was "the pickle in his George Webb hamburger" because the office of the agency through which they adopted me was located on the second floor of a building, above a George Webb Hamburger Restaurant.

Initially, I felt like any little girl in a loving family. I had two older brothers. We had fun, we played, we fought, and we loved each other. My parents provided everything we needed. We were not rich, but we were comfortable.

My father was a high school math teacher and my mother was a housewife until I was 4 years old, when she went back to college to finish her degree in education. They planned it perfectly. My mother started teaching the year I started school.

The summer before I was to start kindergarten, we moved from a small house in town to a farm in the country. We had a bigger house with a bedroom for each of us, two sheds, a granary, a barn and forty-three acres of land on which to run and play. We could ride our bikes along the country roads without worry. There was a lake across the road from our house. In the summer we would go fishing and in the winter we would ice skate on the frozen lake.

I like to refer to our country home as a hobby farm. Even though my parents both taught school full-time, we had horses, steers, pigs, chickens, rabbits, cats and dogs. We also had a huge garden each summer.

Farm life was a family endeavor that required hard work and cooperation. We learned responsibility, love and respect for animals and developed a great appreciation for the value of land.

My father had a wonderful sense of humor and always found a way to make the work seem like fun. One year for Christmas my brothers and I each received a shovel with our name written on the handle. We were happy to have our very own shovels, even though they were to be used to clean up behind the steers in the barn!

In the spring and summer, my father would allow me to do odd chores in order to earn money for rides at the county fair in August. He used to pay me a penny for each rock I picked up from the freshly plowed field. As he drove the tractor, I would walk in front, picking up rocks and throwing them into the bucket on the front of the tractor. Later, as the crops were growing, my father paid me a penny for each goldenrod plant (weed) I pulled out of the field.

My father was also very smart and quite handy. He could fix just about anything as long as he had the manual to read. I loved to spend time with him as he worked on machinery. He would let me hold the light for him, hand him tools, or just laugh as I used a screwdriver to scrape off old dirty grease, thinking I was helping.

We were very close. I was definitely daddy's little girl. I especially enjoyed the times when he would say to me, "Let's go get a piece of pie." Sometimes we would tell my mother we were leaving, and other times we would just hop in the car and drive to the diner in town for a piece of fresh blueberry pie.

Since both of my parents were teachers and all three of us children were in school, the entire family enjoyed it when winter storms blew in and it snowed so much that school was canceled. We lived on an old country road that was typically one of the last to be plowed, and it was fairly common to have snow drifts across the road two to four feet deep.

My dad and I viewed a snow day as a special time. It was as though we had been given a pass to play hooky for the day. We would get bundled up in our snowmobile suits and boots and head out into the winter wonderland for a quarter mile trek up the road to our neighbor's house. The neighbors were a very nice elderly couple, and my father felt the need to make sure they were alright during those times. I loved our winter walks. They were great adventures and I felt like dad and I were out to save the world.

My mother was very loving and talented as well. She was a wonderful cook and a remarkable seamstress. As a matter of fact, she sewed most of my clothes throughout my childhood. I especially loved the beautiful dresses she made me for holidays. She also made the most exquisite gowns for my Barbie dolls. I can't imagine the patience she had to sew such tiny clothes with incredible detail and precision.

Mom and I had our special time together, too. Every Thursday night in the fall and winter, dad and my brothers would go to church to play dart-ball. While they were gone, Mom and I always made a bowl of popcorn and then we would sit on her bed eating it while she read bedtime stories to me.

My mother seemed to be the one who, more often than not, drove my brothers and me to doctor and dentist appointments. My oldest brother, Mike, had thyroid problems. My other brother, Jim, was extremely accident prone and was constantly getting hurt. I had a chronic kidney infection and needed monthly monitoring. Mom had the patience of a saint. I specifically recall one day when I had to be at the doctor's office for a full eight hours. I was having blood drawn every hour for some kind of test. During that time, my mother read the entire book of Charlotte's Web to me.

I loved the fact that my parents were both teachers because it allowed us to have the entire summer together as a family.

One of my fondest childhood memories was the summer when I was seven years old. Our television broke and we did not have the money to fix it or to buy a new one. We had to entertain ourselves instead of just zoning out in front of the TV. Quite often we played baseball in the field before dinner and then spent the evening playing cards and board-games as a family. Sometimes we would saddle up the horses and just ride for hours.

My parents gave us every opportunity possible. We were in 4-H, active in our church, and participated in sports at school. Overall, we were raised in a very wholesome and loving environment.

This sounds like an idyllic life, and in most ways it was, but underneath it all was that initial abandonment, slowly festering and undermining my sense of self-worth. It grew as I grew, surfacing at times and in many ways throughout my childhood.

CHAPTER TWO

Even though I had a wonderful childhood and I knew that I was loved very much by my family, I still felt that I was different because I was adopted. I knew I wasn't a blood relative, but that I was only part of our family legally.

I remember one time when I was about six or seven years old, my oldest brother wanted me to do something for him and I said, "No." He teased me, saying, "If you don't, I won't love you anymore." My response to him was, "You have to love me because I'm legal!" My dad thought my comeback was great and has told that story many times. But, that was my perception. I knew that my mom had given birth to my brothers so they were blood relatives, but I wasn't. I was part of the family by law.

At family events, I was always the one who stood out. My mom had three brothers and one sister, each of whom had several children, so family gatherings were busy and full of life. My dad used to say you could tell right away which child was adopted because my brothers and all my cousins had sandy blond hair, but my hair was almost black.

I remember that when I was little, my dad used to tease me about how little I looked like my brothers and cousins.

"What happened to the blue-eyed, blond I ordered?" he'd ask. "You know, I tried to take you back and trade you in for a new model with blue eyes and blond hair, but when I got there, they said I had too many miles on you, so I would have to keep you."

Despite the fact that he always followed up this joking by scooping me up into his arms and hugging me, a part of me always wondered if he actually would have taken me back if a blue-eyed blond child had been available. Just the idea that I wasn't exactly what he had ordered was scary to me.

Quite often, I would look in the mirror attached to my dresser and imagine how I'd look if I had blonde hair and blue eyes. I used to wonder who I looked like. Did I look like my birth mother or biological father? Were there any other children out there who looked like me?

I knew that I was lucky to have been adopted. I also knew that I could never be a blue-eyed blond like my brothers and cousins. Since I couldn't control my physical features, I tried to be perfect in other ways like keeping my bedroom spotless and getting straight A's in school. Everything I did had to be "just so."

By the time I was in second grade, I was seeing a psychologist. I had become lethargic and my parents thought I might be depressed, so they had me evaluated. As it turned out, the lethargy was not from depression. Instead it was from a new medication I was taking for my chronic kidney infection. In the process of the evaluation, however, the psychologist determined that I was a perfectionist. He told my parents that if we didn't resolve the problem then, it could become a huge issue later on in life. He said children like me were the type who were more likely to commit suicide in high school or college when life became challenging and they were not able to control everything in their environment.

So, I went to counseling once a week for several months. All I remember about it is that the counselor and I would play checkers. On the first visit he let me win, but never again. I'm sure he talked to me too, but I don't remember any of that - just that I didn't like to lose at checkers! I guess the counseling helped me to relax and not be such a perfectionist, but it didn't change how I really felt.

It seems to me that my impressions of adoption and of myself really started to shift when I was in grade school. Being exposed to so many other children was great, but I soon realized that I was the only one in my class who was adopted. As a matter of fact, I was the only adopted person I knew until I was in high school.

I often wondered what it would feel like to be my parent's biological child. I imagined that it must feel different - more complete in some way - when you are raised by your biological parents.

Even writing about how different I felt as a child makes me feel guilty . . . like I wasn't appreciative enough.

But I was constantly being reminded that I was lucky to have a family at all – something other children my age could just take for granted. I must always be grateful that I was fortunate to have been chosen while other children were just born into their families.

The adoption agency had recommended that my parents always tell me the truth about being adopted, so I grew up with that knowledge. When I was old enough to understand what being adopted was, I also realized that it meant that my birth mother had given me away.

I felt like I wasn't good enough to have been kept. Something must be wrong with me if my own birth mother didn't want me. How can any child develop a healthy self-esteem knowing that they were abandoned by the one person who should have wanted them more than anything?

Everyday situations provided reminders that I was different. I remember grade school classmates asking me how it felt to be adopted. How was I supposed to answer that question? Being adopted was the only life I had known. It had been normal to me, but I was now beginning to understand that it was anything but normal.

There were other reminders, as well. Every time we went to a new doctor or dentist I would have to answer, "I don't know," to all family medical history questions.

In school, when we did family trees, it bothered me that I did not know my true heritage. I had to do the assignment, but it never felt complete to me because it wasn't my family tree. It was my adopted family tree. I wondered what the chart of my biological family would look like. What were the names of my biological mother and father? Did I have any biological siblings? Where had we come from? Was I related to anyone famous?

At home, as I was maturing into a young woman, I was frustrated because my mother was well-endowed, but I did not have her genetic make-up and was lacking in that department. I know it's a humorous saying, but it always hurt a little when my father would say, "Just remember Paula, what the Lord hath forgotten, you can make up with cotton". It was another reminder that I was adopted and apparently not good enough.

I understand now that people were not intentionally trying to hurt me or make me feel different. But how could I not feel that way? I had been given away the day I was born. I hadn't been good enough for my birth mother to keep me. Even though I was surrounded by a family who loved me, I still felt alone and unworthy. I didn't feel whole.

I remember feeling like I was on the outside, looking in at the world of activity and people around me. It was as though I was an island floating in a vast sea, without connection to solid ground. This was especially true when I was a young teenager, but it lasted into high school and even through college.

For example, it always seemed easy for my girlfriends to attract and date boys, but it seemed very difficult for me. The only reason I had a boyfriend in fifth grade was because my best friends had boyfriends, and they made one of the other boys in our class be my boyfriend in order to be part of our group!

Beginning in eighth grade and into my freshman year in high school, I had my first real boyfriend. I was shocked that this boy actually liked me! He really liked me - just for me and for who I was.

I didn't know why at the time, but when we had been dating for several months and he told me that he loved me, I was completely uncomfortable. It was such a weird feeling! I was torn between emotions. I felt joy and elation that he loved me and at the same time, fear and rebellion at those words because I couldn't imagine him being in love with me. I wasn't ready for that! How could he actually love me? I broke up with him right then and there.

The next boyfriend I had lived 100 miles away - a safe distance. That didn't last long either.

I was attracted to many boys in high school, but very seldom were those feelings reciprocated. Maybe it had something to do with the fact that I attended high school in a Norwegian town and a majority of the girls in my class had blond hair and blue eyes. In my mind, that meant that I was inferior.

Imagine my surprise at the end of my senior year when the results of the Raspberry Awards were revealed and I had tied with one of the popular girls in our class for best body! What? I was shocked! If I had such a great body, how come nobody ever asked me out?

Obviously, I did not have very much self-confidence or a very good self-image. My best friend in high school once told me that when she first met me she thought I was stuck-up. That wasn't the case. The truth of the matter was that I was extremely shy around people I did not know very well. It was difficult for me to have a conversation with someone new because I always felt like what I had to say wasn't important or didn't matter.

College was another world. I had come from a small town with a population of less than 300, and there I was in Madison, Wisconsin, on a campus that had upwards of 50,000 students! It was terrifying and liberating! Fortunately, within the first month of school, I literally bumped into Kim, a childhood friend from grade school. We had lost touch with each other for four years because we had gone to separate high schools and yet, here we were as young adults, reunited. I was so grateful for this because she gave me a sense of familiarity when everything else in my world was foreign.

I remember feeling like Kim was my lifeline. Everyone else seemed to know just what to do and how to act. They all seemed to have an abundance of self-worth and confidence, including my friend Kim. I, on the other hand, still felt like a fish out of water. So, I clung to my friendship with Kim and followed her lead.

The first four years flew by and before I knew it I was graduating with a Bachelor of Science Degree in Education, with a focus in Communicative Disorders. I was on my way to becoming a speech-language pathologist.

My college career didn't end there. At the end of my junior year, I found out that I had to have a Master's Degree in order to be a speech therapist. Fortunately, I was accepted to the two year graduate program at Madison.

Chapter Three

I was 22 years old, beginning my first year of graduate school. I should have been elated, filled with excitement and anticipation for this next step in my life. Instead, I felt empty and lost. The void I felt inside, which had been with me since birth, had expanded little by little over the years and was now becoming all consuming. It could no longer be ignored. I was on the verge of becoming an independent adult and finding myself, but something critical was missing.

I remember thinking about how I was at the age where it would be perfectly normal to be getting married and starting a family of my own. Both of my brothers had gotten married when they were twenty-two years old. Personally, I couldn't imagine myself in that role as I still had two years of school left and didn't even have a casual boyfriend, let alone a serious relationship.

I started to wonder more and more about my birth mother. How old had she been when she gave birth to me? Had she been a teenager in high school? Had she been going to college? Or, was she an adult who had to give me up for circumstances beyond her control? What was her situation? Was she even still alive? I had no idea.

As all of those questions began to whirl around in my mind, I continued to wonder if I looked like her. I had thought about that many times in my childhood, but never really gave it much attention because I had such a wonderful family.

Now, though, I realized that in just two years I would be on my own. How could I venture out into the world when I didn't even really know who I was and where I came from?

Who was my birth mother? One can imagine all kinds of scenarios when you are adopted and don't have all the answers. I used to dream of the woman who was my birth mother. Sometimes I would picture a very successful business woman who traveled the world. Other times I would see her as a happy housewife with a family. On the rare occasion I would picture a homeless woman – beaten down by the tragic events in her past - pushing a stolen shopping cart through Central Park.

The summer between my junior and senior years in college I was working as a waitress in a dinner club. During that summer there were three different occasions when people told me that I looked like Linda Carter, the television actress who had played the role of Wonder Woman! What a compliment! Linda Carter was gorgeous. She had long, wavy dark brown hair, brilliant blue eyes and the body of a model. No one had ever said anything like that to me before, but after it happened for the third time, my imagination took off!

Could Wonder Woman (Linda Carter) be my birth mother? How cool would that be? I began to fantasize how wonderful it would be to find out that I was the child of a famous actress! I held onto that fantasy for a year and then it was time to actually find out.

I had heard stories of how other adoptees had located their biological parents and I started to entertain the idea of looking for my birth mother. I hoped that if I found her all my questions would be answered. Maybe then, that void inside - a part of me that felt empty - would finally be filled. And so, the search began.

I called the state adoption agency to find out how to begin the process. They told me I would have to contact the agency through which I had been adopted - an agency that was part of the church organization to which my parents belonged.

Then, I called my parents. As I mentioned, I had a great family! My parents were and are the most generous and loving people I know. I couldn't move forward without their blessing. The last thing I ever wanted to do was to hurt their feelings.

I remember my hesitation and how nervous I was to bring up the subject of finding my birth mother. I'll never forget my surprise and elation at their response. They said, "We support you 100%. We always thought this day would come. It's only natural. We just always hoped you would wait until you were at least eighteen years old so that if you found her, she couldn't take you away from us." My father even offered to help me with a private investigation if my search through the adoption agency was unsuccessful. Wow! How did I get so lucky?

The next step was to call the adoption agency. They told me it was an easy process. I had to fill out an application, send it in and then pay them $50 per hour for the search. The one contingency was that they would have to search for both parents. What? Why? I was only interested in finding my birth mother, not my father. Why would I want to find him? Obviously, he didn't care about me! If he had cared, I wouldn't have been adopted! I could only imagine and believe that he had left my birth mother and that was why she gave me away! But, I had no choice. I had to follow the rules if I wanted to find my birth mother, so I agreed.

I received the application in the mail, but I couldn't fill it out - not for ten months. As soon as I had the application, I was paralyzed. I was afraid. I was afraid of what I might or might not find on the other end. If I found her, what would she be like? Would she want to meet me or would she refuse? What if I found out that I was too late and she had already passed away? What if I couldn't find her at all?

Finally, after months of contemplation, I filled out the application. There was a section on the application which asked for a statement of why I wanted to find my birth mother. It was to be read to her when she was located.

I wrote the following:

I am looking for my birth mother because I want her to know that I am okay. I have had a wonderful life and am currently in graduate school to become a speech therapist. I want her to know that I am not looking for a relationship with her. I don't want to interfere in her life. I want her to know that even though I don't know the circumstances of why I was put up for adoption, I believe she did the best thing for me. I have a wonderful family and I am happy.

It took three months and $150 for the adoption agency to find my birth mother.

CHAPTER FOUR

I'll always remember that crisp spring day in March, 1990. I had just gotten back to my apartment building from class. In two months I would be graduating and beginning my new life - my professional career. I opened my mailbox and there it was: a letter from the adoption agency! My heart was pounding! Was it good news or bad news? I was trembling as I opened the envelope.

I unfolded the letter and read the first sentence:

Dear Paula,

I have good news for you. I have contacted your birth mother...

I skipped to the middle of the page:

Your birth mother is: Pauline.......

Pauline? My name was Paula and hers was Pauline! How did that happen? My first thought was my dad must be psychic! I remembered the story my parents had told me of how they named me. My mom had wanted to name me Elizabeth, but my dad had said, "I think she looks like a Paula." And so it was. They had no information about my birth mother as it had been a closed adoption.

I couldn't think! I wanted to scream out loud, "I found her! I found my birth mother!" I had to tell someone! I clutched the letter and ran to a house at the end of the block where my friend, Kim, lived with her fiancé. I was praying that they would be home, and they were.

I was shaking like a leaf as I handed Kim the letter. I couldn't believe it! I had actually found my birth mother! She wasn't Wonder Woman, but I didn't care. I had a name and an address and now I felt like I could have all my questions answered and fill that void inside.

As soon as I returned to my apartment, I immediately called my parents. They were elated for me when I told them I had found my birth mother and just as shocked as I was that her name was Pauline.

Now the ball was in my court. It was up to me to make the next move, so I wrote Pauline a letter. I told her how exciting it was for me to actually have found her and how grateful I was to have had such a wonderful childhood with a loving family. I reiterated that I had no idea why I had been given up for adoption, but that I was happy - happy for my family and now especially happy for the opportunity to know her. And so began my relationship with my birth mother.

Within a week, I received my first official correspondence from Pauline. She was grateful to know I had had a wonderful childhood in a loving family. She told me that she had never gotten married or had any other children. She lived in northern California and worked in a law firm in San Francisco. She wrote that she had often wondered about how I was doing and was now looking forward to getting to know me. Hopefully, one day, she would meet me in person.

I received that letter from Pauline the first week in April, 1990. The next week, right on April 12, I received a birthday card from her. At first I was surprised. I thought, "How did she know?" Then an instant later I thought, "Well, duh, silly girl. She was there when you were born!" Of course, she, of all people would know my birthday. I was sure she had thought of me every year on April 12.

This all happened during my last semester of grad school. In May, I would be graduating and heading out into the world on my own. I initially wanted to stay in Wisconsin to be close to my family, but couldn't find the kind of job I wanted there.

I had a friend from college who had graduated two years before and had moved to Los Angeles. He and I had kept in touch and he told me I should consider moving to California for a couple years. He was sure I could find a job there and he would help me get established. So, I moved.

My friend, Rick, helped me find an apartment in Hermosa Beach, California. He also helped me put together a budget I could live on and introduced me to all of his friends.

It was overwhelming: graduating from college, moving across the country and starting a new career - not to mention, just having found my birth mother! It took a couple months for me to adjust and get into a routine I could handle.

I stayed in contact with Pauline and by early fall, we were planning a time to actually meet in person. We agreed that I would drive up to San Francisco to see her in October.

I was excited and apprehensive at the thought of meeting Pauline face to face. We had written letters back and forth and had spoken on the phone, but you never really know what a person is like until you meet them and spend time with them. I had dreamt of this my entire life and I didn't want to be let down from the fantasy meeting I had envisioned.

As October drew closer and my trip was just around the corner, I began to feel like I needed support for this first meeting. I did not think I could do it on my own so I asked Rick to join me. He was thrilled and immediately agreed to accompany me. I was relieved when he accepted my invitation. Rick was my entire support system in California. He was my foundation. I felt safe when I was with him and I knew that I could do anything as long as he was by my side.

In the days leading up to the trip, Rick started telling all our friends what an exciting trip it would be. He said to them, "How cool is this? I get to go along and experience a once-in-a-lifetime event when Paula meets her birth mother for the very first time! How many people get to experience something like that? I can't wait. I'm just going to sit back and watch it all unfold!"

Finally, the day arrived and Rick and I started our eight hour drive from Los Angeles to San Francisco. We took the scenic route along the coast. It was breathtakingly beautiful, but all I could think about was meeting Pauline. This was it! There was no turning back now. We were on our way to Pauline's home where we would spend the weekend. As the hours and the miles passed, my anxiety level rose, along with the excitement and anticipation of meeting Pauline.

When we reached San Francisco, I felt like there was a rock in my stomach. We were almost there and my mind was whirling. What will she be like? Will I like her? Will I hate her? Is she wonderful or is she a crazy lady? Will she like me? What will she think of me?

Finally, we reached the exit off the freeway which led to Pauline's home. We were within a mile of her house and I panicked. "Pull over!" I screamed. It was all too real now! Rick turned the car into the parking lot of a store. I got out of the car and started pacing. I felt like I couldn't breathe! Rick got out of the car and came over to me. I said, "Either slap me or hug me because I am freaking out right now! I don't know if I can do this!"

Thank God for Rick in that moment. He wrapped me in his strong arms and told me I would be okay. He reminded me that this was an exciting time, a wonderful opportunity, and that he was there by my side to support me. He promised that we could leave at any time if I felt uncomfortable. After a few minutes and several deep breaths we were back in the car, heading to Pauline's house.

We pulled into the driveway and parked next to the garage. My heart was pounding as I got out of the car. Just then, Pauline looked over the fence of the side patio of the house and said, "There's a face I know!" We had exchanged photos in our letters and that was her ice-breaker. This was the moment I had waited for all my life! It seemed surreal. Somehow, it was as if I was in a slow-motion scene of a movie.

As we entered her house, we were introduced to a married couple, goods friends of Pauline, who were there to support her, just like Rick was there for me. We all sat out on the patio and chatted. Conversation was light and after an hour or so Pauline's friends went home. The entire time, I felt like I was outside of my body. It was as if I was watching the whole thing while floating above the group.

Later that evening, Pauline, Rick and I had a nice dinner and we drank champagne to celebrate this amazing event. Everything was going well, so Rick turned in early to give Pauline and me some time alone.

She showed me pictures of her family and her childhood. Her father had passed away several years prior. However, she still had her mother, one sister and brother-in-law and one niece. It was a very small family but it was my family. Finally, I had blood relatives. I wondered what they were like and imagined how nice it would be to meet them.

Pauline had been raised in a small town in Washington State, where her mother still lived. It seemed like a different world to me as she described it - totally foreign from anything I had experienced growing up.

As I looked at the photos and listened to stories from Pauline's childhood, I began to ask questions. What was her reaction when she found out I was looking for her? How old was she when I was born? Why had she given me up for adoption? Who was my father?

Pauline began by telling me that we almost didn't meet. The adoption agency had called her mother's house, which was the only phone number they had on record. Fortunately, her mother still lived in the same house, with the same phone number, 24 years later. Supposedly, Pauline's mother was very leery about the call. The person from the adoption agency had told her that they had gone to college with Pauline years ago and wanted to get back in touch with her. Pauline's mother was hesitant but finally gave that person Pauline's phone number.

After Pauline received the call from the adoption agency and found out that I was looking for her, she was thrilled and called her mother. Her mother said, "If I had known that it was the adoption agency calling I would never have given them your number!" I guess Pauline's mother thought that she would have been protecting Pauline, but Pauline informed her mother that she was grateful to have heard from me and to have the opportunity to get to know me.

She went on to tell me the story of her pregnancy. She didn't tell me all the details - just that she had gotten pregnant when she was 20 years old and in college. At that time, her family had owned a store in their small town in Washington, and the man who was my father had worked in the store. She told me that he was the first one she called. She told him she was pregnant and that they would have to get married. As the story went, he told her he wouldn't marry her because he had too many other things going on in his life at that time, and that she was on her own.

So, she turned to her parents. Pauline went home one weekend and told her parents she was pregnant and that the father was not going to marry her. She then told me that her parent's first reaction was that they were going to send her half way around the world to Switzerland to have an abortion!

I couldn't believe what I was hearing! Who were these people? How could they possibly think of sending their own daughter away for an abortion? Did they really think they were that important? Was this really such an awful cross for the family to bear? And, what was wrong with me? I was an innocent baby in this process! How could they just discard me like some despicable insect? I felt hurt by hearing that part of the story. I felt like her parents must have been monsters! They certainly could not have loved Pauline very much!

As it turned out, Pauline's parents took her to their family doctor for a physical before putting her on a plane to Switzerland. Thank God, again! The doctor did his exam and told Pauline's parents she was already four months pregnant and could not have an abortion. So, they did the next best thing and shipped her half was across the country to stay with a foster family in Wisconsin for the last five months of her pregnancy! And that's why I was born in Milwaukee, Wisconsin.

I was listening to the story, trying to process all this information and feeling so many emotions. She continued. She said her father had told her that after she gave birth, she was not to look at me or hold me. He said that it would be easier for her to let go that way.

I was in shock! How could her parents have been so cold? I did not understand! Pauline went on to tell me that her parents really were warm, loving people and that they had handled the situation the best way they knew. In 1966, it was considered a total disgrace to a family for a daughter to become pregnant out of wedlock. It was not uncommon for those young, pregnant girls to be shipped away to have their babies so as not to damage the family name. Unreal!

Next, I wanted to know more about the man who was my biological father. Pauline told me that she had dated him for a short period of time the summer before I was born. She said that he still lived in her hometown, the same town where her mother resided. She said she understood that at some point in time I may want to look him up and then she made a request of me.

She asked that I wait to look for my biological father until her mother passed away. She said that she wouldn't want to cause her mother any shame if word got out now about Pauline's pregnancy. I was irritated by that. However, since I had no desire to locate my biological father at that time, I agreed to honor her request.

That was a lot of information for one day. As I lay in bed that night, a multitude of emotions were churning inside me. I felt joy and happiness at finally having met my birth mother. I was grateful to have answers to questions I had wondered about for years. I felt upset and hurt by Pauline's parents. I was angry for the way they had treated Pauline all those years ago. I also felt rejected again. How could they have not wanted me? I was an innocent baby! It wasn't my fault! I tried to rationalize why everything had happened the way Pauline described it, but there was a deep sense of resentment forming inside of me, one that would slowly fester over the next few years.

Overall, the weekend with Pauline in San Francisco was a great experience. Even though I had so many mixed emotions because of the information I had received, I was grateful to finally know the whole story.

As Rick and I drove back to Los Angeles, we reflected on the weekend. "Do I look like Pauline?" I asked. Rick replied, "Yes, you look just like her and it's cool to see her now, at forty-five years old, because if you still look like her when you're that age, you're going to be HOT!" I had to laugh. Only Rick would think of something like that. When I asked him what else he had observed, he said, "You are a perfect balance of genetic versus environmental influence. Now, having met Pauline, I see that you are like her in the ways in which you are different from your family. It's amazing to see both sides."

It was good to have an objective opinion and interesting to hear Ricks thoughts. Maybe, that's why I had always felt happy, but different while I was growing up. I was so blessed to have been adopted into an incredible, loving family, and I knew I had acquired their morals and values. Perhaps now I would begin to understand the rest of me.

CHAPTER FIVE

I lived in Hermosa Beach for two and a half years during which time Pauline and I kept in touch via mail, phone calls and an occasional weekend visit. I'd fly to San Francisco to stay with her. We had fun getting to know each other and I enjoyed seeing the sights in northern California. But it was always just the two of us. Once in a while we would see Pauline's friends who had been at her house the first time we had met, but we never spent time with any of her other friends, which seemed strange to me.

I felt happy in my new found relationship with my birth mother, but I also felt frustrated and disappointed. I naturally wanted to know about her family, and as she and I became close, I wanted more and more to be a part of her family. That wasn't possible.

Pauline told me that her sister and brother-in-law had known of her pregnancy and that I had been given up for adoption. What they did not know was that I had found her twenty-four years later and that we were now developing a relationship.

She told me she couldn't tell them about me because her sister had short term memory deficits and Pauline was afraid that if her sister knew about me now, she may inadvertently say something about me to a family member or family friend. Her fear was that the truth about her pregnancy would become public knowledge in her home town and that would disgrace and hurt her mother.

Pauline also told me that her mother could not bear to see or meet me when she came to California to visit. Pauline said that her mother had asked her to tell me that she loved me, but that she couldn't see me because just thinking about me brought back memories of all the pain and suffering the family had gone through in 1966.

That was incredibly hurtful to me. Part of me was so happy to have Pauline in my life and another part of me was raw with pain because once again, I couldn't be accepted for who I was. I might still bring shame to the family name. So, I took what I could get and decided to just be happy knowing Pauline.

In the fall of 1992, I decided to move back to Wisconsin. I had a wonderful, fun time in California, but I was missing my family. My parents were very happy that I was "coming home" and they decided to fly out to California and drive back to Wisconsin with me. What a great idea! It would be the perfect opportunity for them to meet Pauline.

I drove from Los Angeles to San Francisco and picked up my parents at the airport. Then we headed to

Pauline's house to meet her and spend the night before beginning our trip across the country. I felt like a five year old girl again. Mom and dad were thanking Pauline for giving birth to me and she was thanking my parents for having raised me in such a loving environment. It was a very pleasant meeting.

The next morning we set out for Wisconsin. I was excited to get back home to be closer to my family. I figured that now, at age twenty-six, I was ready to settle down. I finally wanted to get married and start my own family. I thought that since I now knew Pauline and had my questions answered - since I knew who I was and where I came from - I should be able to move forward. Silly me.

I lived in Milwaukee, Wisconsin from November 1992 till August 1995. I had a great time, made a lot of friends, and attended about eight weddings in those two years. I had stayed in contact with friends from college and from California and it seemed to me that they were all getting married now. Not me.

I still didn't even have a serious boyfriend. I dated once in a great while, but I was not a person who attracted a lot of men. I couldn't figure it out. I was tall and thin, with an athletic figure, a wonderful personality and a good job. Somehow, though, deep inside, I really did not believe that I deserved to have what everyone else had because I was different.

I wondered what was wrong with me. Why hadn't I found the right man? I tried not to think about it too much, but I couldn't really let it go. It wasn't fair! Why was it so easy for everyone else, but not me? Why did everyone else find it so easy to attract their perfect mate while I struggled?

Maybe the man of my dreams wasn't in Wisconsin. Maybe, I wasn't meant to settle down close to my family. The only vision I could see for myself was of being alone and becoming an old spinster if I stayed in Milwaukee. Perhaps I really wasn't happy there.

I didn't understand. I had found my birth mother and had a good relationship with her. That should have made me complete. Pauline had even ventured to Milwaukee to visit me and had met my entire family at my grandmother's 75th birthday party. I had the best of both worlds, so why was I still alone and unhappy?

I began to miss the fun and sun in California. I thought to myself that maybe that's where I was really meant to be if I was going to be completely happy. So, in August 1995, I packed my bags and moved back to Hermosa Beach, California. I still had a lot of friends there, including one of my best friends, Becky, who had just gotten married. I stayed with her for the first month until I found my own apartment.

Along with the move came a new career. I had contacted the woman who had been my boss the first time I lived in California. She worked for a national therapy company, and although she didn't have a therapy job for me, she did hire me as an orthotics sales representative. I had twenty-five facilities to cover; thirteen in the Los Angeles area and twelve in northern California.

I spent half my time in the San Francisco area, which gave me a great opportunity to see Pauline again on a regular basis. I even stayed with her when I was there for work.

It was great! I would visit my Los Angeles facilities on Monday and Tuesday; then hop on a plane to San Francisco on Wednesday, rent a car, work for the day and end up at Pauline's for the evening. On Thursday morning, I would get in the rental car, visit more facilities, end my day at Pauline's house, and on Friday, after a few facility visits I would return the car and fly back to Los Angeles for the weekend. Staying with Pauline gave me more time to develop our relationship and it saved my company the expense of a hotel room. It was a win – win situation.

That job lasted for about a year and during one of my trips to San Francisco, I actually had the opportunity to meet my biological grandmother, Paulette. Yes, her name was Paulette. Paulette, Pauline and Paula; what a funny twist of fate.

It had been five years since I had found Pauline, and now, finally, Paulette was open to meeting me. It was an interesting meeting, to say the least.

Paulette was a very proud woman who dressed with style and displayed a great amount of etiquette - almost too much etiquette. I hadn't been raised that way. Yes, I had good manners and I was polite, but that was the extent of etiquette in my family. I remember being uncomfortable around her, feeling like she expected a bit too much from me. At one point in conversation she pointed out that I had nice legs. She said, "Of course you have great legs because you come from good stock." I felt like I was being put through a test for Paulette's approval - like a race horse that was being sized up by a potential buyer. I was both disgusted and irritated.

It seemed to me that Paulette thought she was better than other people. As the weekend progressed I started to see an interesting dynamic in the relationship between Pauline and her mother.

For the first time, I began to see the influence Paulette had over Pauline. Paulette made several comments, stating that even though Pauline had been through the experience of getting pregnant out of wedlock and having to give the child (me) up for adoption, she still loved Pauline. It was weird, almost as if Paulette was still holding that event against Pauline. It seemed like she would not let go and completely forgive her daughter.

Pauline acted differently as well when her mother was with us. The two of them, together, seemed to point out other people's flaws, or lack of etiquette, as if they themselves were perfect. It was eye-opening for me! I began to think to myself how blessed I was to have been adopted into my loving family. I realized that if Pauline had kept me and raised me, I would have become a very different person. I really didn't like the idea of what kind of person I would have been.

I realized that I had been idolizing Pauline. I had been so happy to have met her and to have her in my life that I had put her on a pedestal and had actually thought she could do no wrong. Seeing her with her mother broke that "spell" and allowed me to see her as she really was - just another human being, doing the best she could given the circumstances.

I began to sense a deep-seated pain and anger in her, as if she had never forgiven herself for having put her family through such an ordeal. How could she forgive herself, after all, when her mother never let her forget about it? Again, I felt anger and resentment toward Paulette, and I almost felt sorry for Pauline. That was my only encounter with Paulette.

Shortly after that weekend, I was offered and accepted a consulting position with another nation-wide therapy company which meant my weekly visits with Pauline would come to an end.

I spent the next two years flying all over the country for work and I loved it! I was climbing the corporate ladder, meeting a multitude of wonderful people and seeing and experiencing parts of the US that I had only heard about. I traveled from Boston to Phoenix; Indianapolis to Charleston; New York City to Naples, Florida. I was on top of the world. I stayed in touch with Pauline, flew to Wisconsin two or three times per year to see my family and spent the weekends at home in California.

As they say - whoever "they" are - all good things come to an end. Sometime in the spring of 1998, the small consulting group I was working with was dissolved, and the company transitioned me into a therapy management position at a facility in Inglewood, California. No more airplanes, just Los Angeles traffic! The good news for me was the fact that I actually had a chance to spend more time at home, sleeping in my own bed and not in a hotel. I could spend time with my friends on the weekend instead of unpacking, doing laundry and then packing again for the next flight.

In the fall of 1998 I received a call from Pauline, stating that she was moving back to Washington to be closer to her aging mother. Pauline was still single and felt obligated to be there for Paulette.

Prior to her move, Pauline decided to have a farewell picnic in northern California with her friends and she invited me to attend. I accepted, and when the day came, I was amazed. Pauline actually introduced me to her friends as her daughter! What an enormous breakthrough, I thought! Finally, she had accepted me for who I was and she was willing to admit it to her friends. At last, I felt recognized!

My guess is that Pauline finally felt safe about telling the truth to her California friends because she was leaving. It didn't matter if they still accepted her after she disclosed her secret to them because, technically, she would never have to see them again.

They were all very pleasant to me and we had a wonderful day. I thought this would be a new beginning in my relationship with Pauline. Now, maybe, she had fully accepted me and was no longer ashamed.

The trip back to Los Angeles at the end of the weekend was bittersweet. One part of me was sad that Pauline was moving out of the state and I did not know if or when I would see her again. The other part of me was thrilled to have finally been acknowledged, in public, as her daughter.

CHAPTER SIX

It was December, 1998. I was working as a rehab manager - a very stressful job - and just trying to deal with the rat race of life. One day, I received a call from my friend Julie.

I had initially met Julie two years prior, in Indiana, when I was doing rehab consulting. She was a very energetic, positive person and we hit it off immediately. After finishing my job in Indiana I was sent to Phoenix, Arizona. While I was in there, Julie decided to move to Phoenix and we had another opportunity to work together for a short while. We had kept in touch since that time.

Now, Julie was calling me about a new and exciting business proposition with a custom health company. It was a chance to build my own business by marketing customized vitamins. I saw this as the perfect opportunity to create time and financial freedom for myself and I had the luxury of beginning on a part-time basis, while still working at my full-time rehab job.

I had just begun my new business, which was going well, when in April, 1999, the rehab company I worked for closed their western division. There I was, thirty-three years old, still single, and out of a job! It was a time of uncertainty. I had become frustrated with the rehab industry, so I decided to take a year off and devote all of my energy to building my new business with the custom health company.

Since I was unemployed and had time on my hands, I decided to take a trip home to Wisconsin to see my family for Memorial Day. While I was there, my father said that one of his cats had a new litter of kittens. He said there were three gray kittens and that the mommy cat had just moved them to a wood pile on the lawn which was covered by a tarp.

I made a bee-line to the wood pile to see the new babies. As I approached, I could see the three little fluff balls running around and playing. They were about a month old and as cute as could be. They noticed me when I was just a few yards away and quickly disappeared under the tarp.

I knelt down and lifted the tarp so I could see the kittens. To my surprise, the first thing I saw was not a gray fluff ball, but instead, sitting on a piece of wood and looking at me was the cutest black kitten with a white stripe down her face and chest and four white paws. She stole my heart the second I saw her.

We had always had dogs and cats as pets when I was young but I hadn't had an animal in my life for the past fifteen years. Now, since I was taking a break from the therapy world and was not traveling so much, I decided that I needed to have some unconditional love in my life. I was definitely taking the black and white kitten home to California with me.

By the end of my vacation at my parent's farm, we had found homes for two of the gray kittens and one of my California friends had requested that I bring the third gray kitten home with me so he could give it to his daughter. I told him I would be happy to do so.

The two kittens and I had been back in Hermosa Beach for about a week before my friend was able to arrange a pick up time for the gray kitten. By that time, I realized what a close bond the kittens had to each other. They played together. They slept together. They had been taken from their home and now they found comfort in each other. Plus, I had fallen in love with both of them within that first week.

I spoke with my friend and told him that I could not find it in my heart to separate the kittens and that I wanted to keep both of them with me. He was very understanding and found a different kitten for his daughter.

In the following days and weeks I was very grateful for my new found companions, Madison and Dusty.

I continued to build my home-based business. I lived off my savings, flew to different locations around the country once a month for business seminars, and put a lot of money into my new venture. I loved it! I met so many wonderful people and a whole new world opened up to me.

I finally felt like I belonged. I was working with doctors, chiropractors, naturopaths, dieticians, certified clinical nutritionists and people from all walks of life. It was a wonderful group of like-minded individuals and we all had a common goal.

That first year, my business started with a bang but then quickly fizzled. In early 2000, I was running out of money and racking up credit card debt. One of my California colleagues, also having challenges with her business, told me that she had received some great information from a very wealthy man. He had told her of a seminar we should attend if we wanted to create success in our business. We both signed up for the weekend seminar with great expectations.

That seminar was the beginning of a wonderful transformation for me. There I was, thinking I was going to learn how to build my business when in reality, it was a weekend of personal growth! For the first time in my life I actually realized that I had abandonment issues!

I had always felt a little "different," but now my eyes were wide open! I also realized that I wasn't the only one. Everyone has their own issues, but quite frequently we are not aware of them. I learned that those issues, especially if we don't even know we have them, can hold us back and keep us from true happiness. The key is to become conscious of the issues, and only then can one begin to move forward.

For the first time in my life, I realized it wasn't just my imagination. That little girl inside of me, my inner child, was really hurting. All those feelings were finally validated. I had lived the past thirty-four years, feeling different and putting on a happy face, but deep down, I still wondered what was wrong with me. I felt guilty for having those feelings. After all, I had a great life and had been adopted into a wonderful family, so how could I possibly not be okay? But I wasn't. I had deep emotional scars, and now I was becoming aware of them.

When I got home from the seminar, I called my parents. I had had an epiphany and wanted to share it with them. I finally realized why I had all those unpleasant feelings. I was excited because now I could begin to heal and move forward.

As I told my parents of my weekend awakening, my father asked, "How could any daughter of mine possibly have issues?" I could understand why he would ask that question. He and my mother had opened their home and family to me. They had chosen me. They had given me all the unconditional love any child could hope for. How could I possibly not be 100% okay? He couldn't understand, but I did. It had nothing to do with my adopted family and home. It went back to the womb!

As relieved as I was to finally understand just a small portion of my psyche, what I didn't realize is that personal growth - being aware of your issues and actually working through them - can be a long process, and my journey had only just begun.

Chapter Seven

My year off from work flew by and my home-based business struggled, but I didn't care. I was on a journey of personal growth. I loved hanging out with the positive, happy people I met through my business and learning more about myself. I had grand dreams and visions for my life. I was going to make a million dollars, create financial freedom for myself and open a camp for adopted children to help them with abandonment issues.

So, I kept putting more money into my business, thinking I was doing the right thing. The months passed and the bills got bigger. In May, 2000, I had to acknowledge that my savings were dwindling and I needed to make some money, so I went back to speech therapy part-time.

I still had my home-based business, worked in therapy and was just squeaking by financially. On a trip back to Wisconsin I had the pleasure of spending time with my family and went to one of my niece's basket ball games. As I sat in the stands watching her play, it dawned on me that my priorities were messed up.

Even though I was still single and alone, I had a wonderful family, great parents, brothers and sisters-in-law, three nephews and two nieces. I didn't have children of my own, so why was I wasting time in California when I could be in Wisconsin spending time with the children who were already in my life? I could do speech therapy and still work on my home-based business anywhere. So, in November, 2000, I moved back to Wisconsin yet again.

This time I moved to De Pere, Wisconsin, a small suburb of Green Bay. I was thirty miles from my oldest brother and my nieces and seventy miles from my parents. The best part was that my childhood friend, Kim, who had been my lifeline in college, lived in Green Bay with her husband and three young children. They too, were like family.

I thought to myself that now I would finally settle down, meet the man of my dreams, get married and live life like everyone else. But, I wasn't like everyone else.

Even though I had acknowledged the fact that I had abandonment issues, that didn't really solve anything. I spent all my time outside of work with my family and friends. I didn't go on one date. I was still alone and searching for happiness.

The summer of 2001 was unbearably hot and humid. The weather was just plain miserable and so was I. I began to think about how nice and cool the summers were in California. I even contemplated moving back there for the third time, but it wasn't the same. A lot of my friends had gotten married and moved to other states. The only close friend I had left in California was Becky, and she was starting her own family. Plus, the cost of living in California was outrageous! Still, something inside of me was calling me back to the southwest.

One day toward the end of July, I was talking with my friend, Julie, who had introduced me to my home-based business and still lived in the Phoenix area. I told her how unhappy I was and that I wanted to move back to the southwest, but not to California again. She asked, "Why don't you come to Arizona?" Interesting idea!

Arizona was in desperate need of speech therapists and Julie and I could work on our home-based business together. Julie found me a great apartment and by September 1, 2001, I was living in Chandler, Arizona.

It was a new beginning for me, filled with promise. I still kept in touch with Pauline, who was tending to her ailing mother in Washington State. I worked full-time in speech therapy and spent my evenings working on my business, which was still struggling. I attended weekly meetings and weekend seminars to build my business. What I couldn't figure out was why my business wasn't growing like everyone else's.

In October, one of my mentors hired a married couple to do a weekend seminar on business building and network marketing. Of course I attended because I wanted more information on how to make my business successful.

The main speaker's name was Robert. As I sat in the audience, listening, it seemed like I was the only person in the room and Robert was speaking directly to me! Everything he said rang true to me. It was as if he already knew everything about me and the way my business was growing or not growing. I was amazed!

Toward the end of the day, Robert mentioned that he and his wife offered one-on-one business coaching for people who were interested. As soon as the seminar was over, I made a beeline to Robert and hired him as my coach. I had no idea what I had just gotten myself into!

Since Robert lived in California, we arranged to have a one-hour phone call each week for our coaching session. Our first conversation was not what I expected. Robert asked me to tell him about my life. He wanted to know about my childhood, my family, and all of my past relationships.

I thought he was crazy, and so I was initially hesitant to divulge my personal information. I asked him what that had to do with building my business. He responded that he needed to know about my past in order to figure out why I was not allowing my business to grow. Was he insinuating that I was the problem? I certainly did not think that was the case. However, I went along with the program and proceeded to tell him all about myself.

When I told him about my dating experience, he asked, "Why haven't you been married yet?"

I responded, "I seem to always attract men who will not commit to me."

I was shocked at his response. He asked, "Who do you really think is the one with the commitment problem? You are the common denominator in each of your relationships, and therefore, you are the one with the commitment problem!"

What?! It couldn't be me! I was sure of it! I had committed to many things in my life, like college. Not only had I made it through undergraduate school; I also completed two years of grad school! That takes a serious commitment! I thought for sure he was wrong.

My lack of a serious relationship had to have been either the men I dated or the fact that I had moved back and forth across the country five times in the twelve years since college. At that time I couldn't see the truth – the fact that my commitment challenges were in fact tied to my underlying belief that I was not good enough – a result of having been abandoned at birth. I was speechless.

Robert went on to give me my first assignment by challenging me to commit to something I enjoyed. I told him that I liked to exercise.

"OK," he said, "Then you will exercise for thirty minutes every day for the next seven days. Will you commit to that?"

I immediately bucked the system by telling him that I didn't think thirty minutes was a very good workout and that I would rather work out for at least one hour, four times within the next seven days.

He replied, "No. You can exercise for more than thirty minutes if you choose, but you WILL work out for at least thirty minutes EVERY DAY for the next seven days. Do you commit?"

Finally, I agreed.

He then went on to say, "Good. Now, you will also agree that if you do not exercise every day for the next seven days, you will sign a check for $150 and send it to me and I will donate it to the charity of my choice. Do you agree?"

I had no choice. I had to work out every day! I couldn't afford an extra $150!

I made it through six of the seven days before I became physically ill.

I was dreading my next call with Robert. I was sure I would be writing out a check for money I did not have. As it turned out, there was a lesson to be learned. Robert did not collect the extra money, but he did explain to me that I had actually made myself sick because I had such an aversion to commitment. That was an eye opener!

We continued with the commitment to exercise for the next week, plus added another commitment having to do with marketing my products for my business.

As the weekly calls with Robert progressed, so did my list of commitments. After about a month, Robert asked me for some of my goals.

Something I had on my list was to complete a marathon. I had chosen the Big Sur marathon in California and had actually begun training for it the year before. But of course, per my subconscious aversion to commitment, I had been injured with a pulled muscle in my thigh and had to stop training. That had been at the end of 2000 and now we were fast approaching the end of 2001.

The Big Sur marathon is always held in April. I had five months to train, so I signed up for the marathon, put together a training schedule and started running. I also kept up my weekly calls with Robert and continued to work on my business building.

Interestingly, I did not join a running club in order to train for the marathon. Instead, I chose to train alone. I had never been a person who enjoyed team sports. I think it was because I didn't feel like I was good enough and didn't want the team to depend on me. I had only participated in individual sports like track and field.

I'm sure that completing the long training runs would have been easier if I had been part of a group, but that didn't work for me. This was something I had to do on my own.

Running became therapeutic for me. It was a time when I could lose myself and not think about life, just about the next step. In order to make it through the long runs, I began to chant affirmations to the cadence of my steps. I would chant things like, "I feel great! I could run all day, at this very comfortable pace." As the length of the training runs increased, I came up with new affirmations to keep me motivated, like, "Running in the dirt will prevent any hurt," and "Running in the grass will tighten up my ***!" (You can fill in the blank, I'm sure.) On windy days I would chant, "I love the breeze. It helps me run with ease." This list of affirmations grew with each run.

On April 28, 2002, I completed the Big Sur marathon, 26.2 miles, in 4 hours and 38 minutes! I had committed to the process and had accomplished my goal. Robert was proud of me, but more importantly, I was proud of myself. I now believed that I could do anything as long as I had a plan and took consistent action while remaining committed to the outcome. It was just one of many lessons learned through my coaching with Robert.

I always took a lunch break at work and sat in my car while speaking with Robert for our weekly calls. I remember one specific coaching session. It was a hot day in June, about 115 degrees.

On that particular day, Robert said, "I want you to look into the mirror of your car visor. Look deeply into your own eyes and say, 'Paula, I love you.'"

I flipped down the visor, opened the flap to the mirror, looked deep into my own eyes, and immediately burst into tears! I couldn't do it! I didn't love the person I was seeing in the mirror! All I could see was someone who wasn't good enough!

"I can't do it!" I exclaimed, through uncontrolled sobs and tears.

"Yes you can and you will," prompted Robert.

Finally, in a whisper, and not believing it at all, I mumbled, "Paula, I love you," while barely glancing in the mirror.

Another epiphany! For years I had been aware of the fact that I had abandonment issues and that I had always felt different. More recently, I learned that I had commitment challenges, especially with men, because I didn't feel that I was good enough.

But now, for the first time, I realized that I didn't like "ME!" I didn't like or love me for the person I was. It was a crushing feeling, but finally, I had gotten to the ROOT of the problem.

I was a thirty-five year old woman - possibly half way through my life - and just now uncovering and revealing the truth that had held me hostage from true happiness. It was just another layer of the onion being peeled away, but this one was especially painful. According to Robert, we were finally getting somewhere.

The coaching calls continued, as did the exercises. I would come to learn that part of true growth and acceptance comes from forgiveness: forgiving others who have hurt you, as well as and just as important as, forgiving yourself.

One of the exercises Robert assigned to me was to write a letter of forgiveness to Paulette, my biological grandmother. I was to write out all of my feelings of pain and anger toward her, and at the end, I was to forgive her. He pointed out that Paulette was only human and had done the best she could, given the circumstances. After the letter was written I was to burn it and release the energy to the Universe.

I had completed a similar exercise in that initial personal growth seminar I had attended in California. The task at that time was to write out a painful story from childhood. Once we had our letters written, we paired up with someone from the group and read our letters out loud to our partner. The partner's job was to listen, but to have no reaction. At the end of the reading, the partner was to simply say, "Thank you for sharing."

The fact that the partner gave no reaction to the story was important because there was no feedback to validate the pain the reader was feeling. The reader was to read the story over and over again, with no reaction from the partner, until the time came when the story could be read without emotion from the reader. Eventually, the story held no emotional power for the author. It was an amazing exercise!

I decided to write the letter to Paulette, as Robert had suggested. It was extremely emotional for me. I held so much anger and resentment toward Paulette. I felt completely abandoned by her and I blamed her for Pauline having to give me up for adoption. My body shook with uncontrollable sobbing and my hands trembled as I wrote that letter.

When the letter was completed I was an emotional wreck! I decided that I could not just burn the letter. Instead, I felt like I had to go through the process of reading the letter out loud to someone who would not respond in order for me to release the emotional pain attached to the story. My only challenge was that I had no one to read it to, so I decided to read it out loud to my cat, Dusty.

As I read the letter to Dusty, she backed away. I followed, and continued to read. Again, she backed away, and again I followed and kept reading. Dusty literally ran from room to room as I read the letter to her. I couldn't stop. I had to get that emotional pain out of me. I sobbed and read and followed Dusty. Eventually, she squeezed herself under my dresser to get away. I was still filled with so much pain that I sat on the floor by the dresser and kept reading the letter over and over, until the pain was gone and I was drained. Then I burned the letter.

Two weeks later I found a tumor on Dusty's ear. I took her to the vet and had it biopsied. It was a very aggressive form of cancer and the vet said we had to cut her ear off!

It was then that I realized that Dusty had absorbed all the emotion I had released from the letter to Paulette, but she had no outlet. The only way she could release it from her body was in the form of cancer.

I couldn't fathom the thought of cutting her ear off, so I contacted a homeopathic vet I had met through my custom health business. We opted to treat her with homeopathy and the tumor stopped growing. Dusty went on to live another seven years. It was quite a lesson for me.

Yet another "A-ha" moment in my coaching process came through a conversation with Robert regarding my finances. I had created a large amount of credit card debt because I kept buying products through my home-based business instead of recruiting new team members to leverage my income.

It all went back to the fact that I had such low self-esteem and self-worth. Because I didn't like myself, I needed other people to like me in order to feel good about myself. I had a pattern of putting all my money into my business in order to have my team leaders think I was a "team player," which in my mind, meant that they would like me. It sounds warped, I know, but that's what I was doing. I was a people-pleaser because that was the only way I thought people would accept and like me.

So, in that final conversation with Robert, he told me that I could no longer afford his coaching and that I had to decide whether I was going to build my home-based business with 100% effort or go back to speech therapy full-time to pay my bills.

I was at a point in my life where I felt like I was on overload. I was awakening through my personal growth process and realizing I had come a long way, yet there was still so much to work through. I decided at that time to release my home-based business, continue with speech therapy full-time, and continue to work on "Me." My goal was to get to the place where it would be comfortable and even fun to look in the mirror, stare deeply into my own eyes, smile, and say, "Paula, I truly love you!"

That process would take another four years - with continued focus on personal growth, attending seminars and spiritual retreats, hypnotherapy and meeting and working with mentors/life coaches along the way. I was definitely on the right road, headed in the right direction, but still unprepared for all of the bumps, twists and turns ahead.

Chapter Eight

It was mid-October, 2002, when I received an unexpected phone call. A few days prior, Pauline had called to tell me that Paulette had passed away. Now, Pauline was on the phone again with a question for me.

She asked, "How would you like to go on a cruise to Alaska with my sister, my brother-in-law and myself?"

I responded, "I didn't think they knew about me."

You see, I had known Pauline for twelve years already and she had never told her sister and brother-in-law that I had found her.

"They do now, and they want to meet you!" she replied.

It was poetic justice. I had been kept a secret from the family so as not to disgrace Paulette. Now that Paulette had passed on, Pauline was free to tell the rest of the family about me. She and her family decided to use some of their inheritance to pay for a cruise for the four of us. So, ironically, Paulette paid for me to meet the family.

We had a great trip - a seven day cruise through the inside passage of Alaska in June. It was so wonderful to finally meet the people I had heard so much about and to be welcomed into their family. Still, it was a little awkward for me because my "family" was my parents and brothers in Wisconsin and now Pauline and her family were opening the door for me to be part of their world. Fortunately, they understood. Although I was grateful to now know all of them, the people held in my heart as true family were the people who had raised me. The cruise ended and we went back to our own lives.

Another unexpected call came from my friend Julie, in September, 2003.

She said, "Paula, I met the man you are going to marry."

"Oh, really," I asked. "What makes you think so?"

"Well, he's tall, successful, really nice, and has a great sense of humor! You have to meet him. I'll give him your number if it's okay with you," she replied.

Of course I said yes. Who wouldn't? I was still single, not dating anyone and the biological clock was ticking! Plus, I valued Julie's opinion and trusted her judgment.

A few days later, Tim called me. It was an intense, interesting conversation. He started with something like, "Hi. I'm Tim. I got your number from Julie. Before we get into a conversation, I just have to know how you feel about going out with a guy who is 6'2" and bald. If you have a problem with that, tell me now. And, I'll tell you that if you are 4 feet tall and 4 feet wide, I'm not going to be attracted to you."

That was about as straight forward as it gets!

He went on to say, "I will also tell you that you should ask me as many questions as you want during this call, because this will be the longest conversation we will ever have on the phone. I talk on the phone all day for work and after work I don't want any part of it."

I almost hung up right then and there, but decided to go with the flow because Julie had given him such rave reviews.

As the conversation continued, Tim softened a little and we did have a nice chat. What made me decide to actually meet him was the choice he offered for our first date. We could either meet for drinks some evening, or I could join him on Saturday morning when he did his monthly volunteer work at a home for mentally handicapped adults. He went there once a month and played kickball with the group. I opted for kickball and that was the beginning of our relationship.

I had a great time getting to know Tim. We had several things in common. We both liked college football and went to every ASU home game that fall. We enjoyed going to the movies and loved to travel. Within the first year of our relationship, we went to California, Wisconsin, and Hawaii for long weekends and to Costa Rica for a week.

Traveling with Tim was always an adventure because he didn't like to travel the way everyone else did. Instead, he preferred to be "off the beaten path".

61

For example, when we were in Hawaii we did not stay in a hotel in Honolulu like most tourists. Instead, we stayed at a state park on the northeast side of the island in a yurt! We had a blast meeting the local people who would camp in the park for the weekend and fish all day and all night. They were very friendly and invited us to join them for their meals. What a great way to experience true Hawaiian food! The other advantage was the fact that the beach was about a mile long, with beautiful white sand, and there were only a handful of people there at any given time.

When we were in Costa Rica, we did not stay at the popular resorts on the west coast. Instead, we hired a driver to take us to a small village just north of the Panama boarder on the east coast. There, we stayed in a jungle house with all the creatures that come with that type of setting. Howler monkeys and sloths lived in the trees above, lizards scurried through the house, roaches scattered when the lights were turned on, and Yellow Web spiders, the size of the palm of my hand, spun webs everywhere.

We went on a guided jungle tour with a native gentleman and saw one of most poisonous snakes in the area which was only about a foot long and when curled up on a tree branch, blended in and looked like a knot of wood. We were also up close and personal with a colony of Bullet ants. They lived in the ground at the base of a tree. When the guide banged on the tree trunk, the Bullet ants emerged in droves! Needless to say, there was never a dull moment when hanging out with Tim.

The one thing I loved most about my relationship with Tim was the fact that we were both adopted! Tim was the youngest of three children in his family, all of whom were adopted. I thought to myself, "This is it! I have finally attracted a man into my life who can fully and completely understand me and all of the feelings I have had throughout my life. This is definitely the man with whom I was meant to spend my life."

We did, however, have different opinions about being adopted. Tim said he would never look for his biological parents - not because he didn't want to, but because he felt it would be disrespectful and hurtful to his adoptive parents. I guess that was just the difference in the relationship he had with them versus the relationship I had with my parents. I don't imagine it was fun for my parents when I chose to look for Pauline. However, they were always supportive of my decision, and I had done so with their blessing.

It was sometime around the one year mark in our relationship when I was faced with a major decision. Tim and I were together one evening, having a nice time, when out of the blue, he turned to me and said, "Just so you know, I am never having children."

That hit me like a ton of bricks! I couldn't believe what I had just heard! I had always thought I would have a family. I was already thirty-eight years old. Oh sure, I knew I was at an age when any pregnancy would be high risk, but I was healthy. I had had a wonderful life and was truly ready to settle down and start my family.

I had to think about that for a while. It took a couple of weeks with some deep soul searching on my part. Was I really going to give up on that dream? I had been conditioned to believe that a woman was supposed to have children. It was only natural to assume that when you met "the one," you would get married and have a family.

I was also dealing with the pressures of my family - not my parents or brothers, but extended family members who always had something to say about me still being single. One aunt and uncle in particular would comment every time I saw them. They would say things like, "When are you going to get married and have children? What's wrong with you? Won't any man have you?"

Eventually, I came to the conclusion that I would rather have Tim as a husband - a partner to spend the rest of my life with, than to let him go and be alone again. So, we kept dating.

A couple of months later, Tim said he had been thinking and wanted to talk to me. I was excited. I immediately thought this meant we would be taking our relationship to the next level. Maybe we would get engaged. Maybe we would move in together.

Instead, what Tim had to say was that he thought it was time for me to stop wasting my money on rent and start building equity in a place of my own. He thought I should buy a condo!

Again, I was floored! Now there were two issues slapping me in the face. One was the fact that this relationship was obviously not moving in the direction I had envisioned. The other issue was my own fear. In my mind, buying a home was permanent. I felt like it would strip me of my freedom. If I bought my own place, I would have to be here forever! Again, I was dealing with my commitment challenges. I had always said that I must have a little bit of Gypsy in me because I liked to move every couple years, sometimes from apartment to apartment and sometimes across the country.

It took some coaxing on Tim's part and some heart-to-heart conversations with close friends, but eventually, I realized that it wouldn't be the end of the world. It did make good financial sense. People bought and sold houses all the time. If I really didn't like it or felt the need to leave, I could always sell my place and move. So, in December, 2004, I bought a condo in Chandler, Arizona. I settled in and life went on.

It was a nice evening, sometime in the spring of 2005. Tim and I were at my condo. We had a tasty dinner and then watched a movie. After the movie was over, Tim turned to me and said, "I've been thinking a lot, and I have to tell you that I have decided that I am never going to get married; not to you or anyone else. I have seen too many of my friends get married and then get divorced, and it is awful! I never intend to get divorced, and the only way to make sure that doesn't happen is to never get married."

All I could say was, "SERIOUSLY?" I felt like I had given up everything for this man! I had given up the dream of having children. I had given up my freedom by buying the condo. Now, here he was, telling me that he was never going to get married! Was this some kind of sick joke?

My stomach was in knots. I couldn't breathe. For a long time I was silent, with tears welling up in my eyes. Finally, I looked at him and said, in a very quiet voice, "Then I guess you are not the man for me."

CHAPTER NINE

I was devastated over the break-up with Tim. The only way I knew how to handle it was to talk to my closest friends. Fortunately, they were very supportive and willing to listen.

I have always believed that we are given "signs" in life, and that's exactly how I took it when, in the course of one week, two of my good friends, who didn't know each other said the same thing to me. They each said, "I wonder if your challenge with finding the right guy for you has anything to do with the fact that you never found your biological father. Maybe this is the time to do so."

Could that really be part of the issue? I had never cared about finding my biological father. I had blamed him for abandoning my birth mother – causing me to be put up for adoption, and Pauline had confirmed it. Could that thought process have been holding me back in my own romantic relationships all these years? How?

Maybe there was some validity to it. Maybe this was the time to find him. There was nothing stopping me now. Pauline had requested that I wait to find him till after Paulette passed away, and I had honored that request.

I called my friend Julie and asked for her assistance because I had no idea how to start. I did know his name, though, as Pauline had given me that information when I had first met her. For the purpose of this story, I'll just call him Brad. Pauline had also told me that he lived in the same small town where she had grown up, but that was fifteen years ago. Who knew if he still lived there?

Julie was great. She was much more computer literate than I, and she said she would do an internet search for him.

The next day, I was in the grocery store when my phone rang. It was Julie.

"I found your father," she said.

I almost dropped the phone! That was fast!

"Are you sure?" I asked.

She went on to tell me that she was positive it was him. She had found thirteen men in the state of Washington with the same name, but only one in Pauline's home town. Julie had even called his house to see if she had found the right man.

She went on to tell me that when she called Brad's home, a woman had answered. Julie had asked to speak with Brad, but he was not home at that time. The woman on the phone was Brad's wife and asked Julie who she was. Julie didn't want to tell her that she was my friend and that I was looking for him, so she told Brad's wife that she was a friend of Brad's from high school and wanted to get in touch with him. She told Brad's wife that her name was Pauline! Brad's wife said to Julie, "Yes, you have the right Brad. As a matter of fact, I remember you. I was just a year behind you in school." Julie didn't know how to respond, so she just said that she would call back some other time and hope to catch Brad when he was at home.

I couldn't believe Julie had used Pauline's name! But, at least it had served the purpose and verified that we had found the right man - my biological father.

Julie gave me the phone number and suggested that I call when I felt like it and that I could then explain the initial call from "Pauline."

I finished my shopping and headed home. I couldn't believe that I had Brad's phone number! I made and ate dinner, all the while wondering what it would be like to speak with my biological father for the first time. I couldn't wait any longer. I had to call and talk to Brad. I picked up the phone and dialed the number. It rang once, twice, three times, and then, a woman answered.

I said, "Hi, I'd like to speak with Brad please."

"He's not here right now. Can I ask who is calling?" she replied.

All of the sudden I wanted to scream into the phone, "This is Brad's daughter!" I didn't care what she would think. I didn't care what kind of a shock it would be for her. Brad should have thought about that thirty-nine years ago when he left Pauline high and dry! I was overcome with anger and just wanted to explode!

I hung up the phone without saying another word. I was shocked at myself - at the overwhelming feelings that were spewing forth! Where did all of this anger come from? Had I been carrying these feelings inside of me for my entire life? Why had they suddenly surfaced with such force now? Were all of these emotions somehow connected to my inability to sustain a meaningful romantic relationship? I didn't know how to handle it.

The next day I picked up the phone again, but not to call Brad. This time I called one of my mentors named Phil. I had met Phil at one of the personal growth seminars I had attended years ago. He had been a speaker and had demonstrated a technique for using affirmations to work through challenges in your life. For some reason, I knew he would be the one who could help me with this situation.

I told Phil the story and he was wonderful. He said what I was experiencing was natural and that it was a good opportunity for me to "grow" and to forgive. He agreed to work with me and so I hired him as my coach. We spent the next month working together. Through the use of affirmations, I was able to eventually release my anger toward Brad and come to a place of forgiveness.

Eventually, I was ready to contact Brad again. Phil suggested that I not call Brad, but that I write him a letter, explaining who I was and why I wanted to find him and to also explain about the odd phone calls from Julie and me.

So I wrote Brad a letter. I told him that I believed he was my biological father. I explained that I had done a legal search for Pauline and had found her in 1990, and that she had told me about him. I told him about my promise to Pauline to not look for him until Paulette had passed. I explained that I was interested in knowing him, but that I did not want to interfere with his family life. I also told him about how Julie had helped me locate him and that the two phone calls several weeks prior were really from us.

I put the letter into an envelope, addressed it and mailed it. Now the ball was in his court. All I could do was to wait and hope for a response.

I didn't have to wait too long. About a week and a half after I mailed the letter, I received the call I had been waiting for. It was Brad.

There was no anger, only joy in me. I was speaking with my biological father! He had received the letter and had discussed it with his wife and two grown children. He said that it was very possible that he was my father.

We had a nice conversation. I told him all about my family and my relationship with Pauline. He told me about his family. He said that years ago, he had told his wife about the possibility of him having a child "out there somewhere," so when the letter came, even though it was shocking, it was not a total surprise. He seemed like a very nice man.

That first call with Brad was wonderful. Before we hung up, we agreed that at some point in time, it would be nice to meet each other and decided to talk again in a week or two.

I was on top of the world! I had a great family, I knew my birth mother, and now, I had a chance to know my biological father. This all happened sometime in May or June, 2005, shortly after the break-up with Tim.

Anyone who knows Phoenix in the summer knows that it is HOT! I never liked living in the desert in the summer and was always looking for a way out. Now that I had made contact with Brad, I wanted to meet him and thought it might be a good time for a trip to Washington. A few years prior, Pauline had moved from the Seattle area back to her home town, so ironically, she and Brad were in the same location.

The wheels in my mind started spinning, and I thought about how nice it would be to see Pauline again and be able to meet Brad and his family. I didn't have much vacation time, so, on a whim, I decided to look for opportunities as a traveling speech therapist in Washington.

Remember how I mentioned that I believe in "signs?" Well, as it turned out there was a traveling speech therapy job available in the very town where Pauline and Brad resided! We'll just call it Cedar Point.

I couldn't believe it! But I knew it was meant to be! That job was going to be mine and I was meant to go to Washington! Now all I had to do was to call Pauline and tell her that I had located Brad and that I wanted to come to Cedar Point for three months to work, to see her and to meet Brad.

Pauline was thrilled to hear that I was thinking of taking the job. I hadn't seen her in a couple years and it would be wonderful to spend time together again. She did not, however, want anything to do with seeing Brad again, but supported my wish to do so. She even offered to have me stay with her. She was renting a house that had a finished basement and said I could stay there with my two cats while she and her two cats lived upstairs in the main portion of the house.

I called the traveling therapy company, got the job and secured a speech license in Washington. Then I started making plans for the trip. I was to begin the job in Cedar Point in mid-August.

A couple of days later, Pauline called me. She said, "I've been thinking about your trip here. I am excited to see you again, but I have to tell you that I still value my privacy. The women here with whom I am friends were also friends with my mother, so when we see them I am going to introduce you as my friend."

I couldn't believe what I was hearing! I thought about it for a few seconds and then replied, "Well, the people for whom I will be working know that I am coming there to stay with my birth mother and that I am also going to meet my biological father. That's what I told them when they asked me why I would want to take the job in Cedar Point. They don't know you and don't care who you are, so that shouldn't be a problem. You can introduce me any way you want to, but I have to say that if someone asks me point blank about who I am in relation to you, I will not lie."

We agreed.

I hung up the phone in disbelief. All the feelings of abandonment came flooding back. Once again, I was being denied by my own birth mother. Logically, I could see her point and respect her feelings, but that didn't make me feel any better. It was just plain hurtful.

As I thought more about what Pauline had said, I realized that she was fooling herself if she believed that people wouldn't know who I was. How could anyone possibly think I was just Pauline's friend? I was twenty years younger than her, I was going to be living with her, and I looked just like her! But that was Pauline's issue and she would have to be the one to deal with it.

Over the course of the next month, I had several conversations with Brad and his wife. They were thrilled that we were going to have the chance to meet each other and we were developing a nice relationship.

Then, one day in July, Brad called again. He said he had been thinking about my trip and he was excited about it, but that he had one request. He said that he wanted to do a DNA test to be sure he was my father. I didn't have a problem with that. I completely understood his feelings. He said he would take care of ordering the test and that he would pay for it. I agreed. We took the test and sent it in for evaluation.

I went about my business. I quit my job in Arizona, sublet my condo, and was getting ready for my adventure to Cedar Point.

Three days before I was supposed to leave, my phone rang. When I answered, Brad was on the line.

He said, "Paula, I received the results of the DNA test and I am NOT your father."

My heart sank and my body was numb. I didn't feel anything. I sat down on the couch and asked, "Are you sure?"

I think he actually started to cry. His wife was on the line as well. He said he would email me the results, but that they indicated with 99.99% certainty that he was not my father.

My response was, "Well, then I guess Pauline has some explaining to do."

The news that Brad was not my biological father was disappointing. After speaking with him, I immediately called Pauline. If Brad wasn't my father, who was?

I got Pauline on the phone and explained to her that Brad and I had taken a DNA test and that he was not my father.

I said to her, "Let's do the math. You told me you dated Brad in August, but if you carried me for a full nine months and I was born in April, then you must have gotten pregnant in July, 1965. Who were you with during that time?"

There was silence. After what seemed like forever, in a very quiet voice, Pauline said, "I was in summer school that year and had a couple one-night stands. I can't tell you who your father is."

Surprisingly, I was able to accept that answer. I would never know the true identity of my biological father. However, going through the process of thinking it was Brad, finding him, and dealing with all the emotions that came up for me had been a blessing. I had been able to release the anger and pain I had harbored toward the man who was my father, whoever he may have been.

Unfortunately, the same was not true for Pauline. She had spent thirty-eight years believing Brad was my father. She and her family had avoided him and thought ill of him all those years. Now she was faced with the fact that all of that negative energy had been for naught.

I could hear the fear and worry in her voice as she asked, "Are you still coming to Cedar Point?"

I think my response surprised her.

"Of course I am," I replied. "I quit my job and sublet my condo, and I have a contract with the traveling company. Look, I was excited about meeting Brad and having a chance to get to know him. But, the fact that he is not my biological father doesn't mean that I don't want to spend the time with you. I am still coming to Cedar Point and you and I are going to have a great time!"

Her sigh of relief was audible.

Three days later, I packed my car and my cats and headed to Washington.

CHAPTER TEN

Cedar Point was beautiful in August. It was a quaint town with a population of around 15,000 residents and was nestled on the side of a mountain, overlooking the ocean. There were evergreen and deciduous trees everywhere. It was very lush and the weather was cool, and I was thrilled to be out of the stifling heat of Arizona.

I settled into my space in the basement of Pauline's house and started my speech therapy job at the local nursing home.

I was one of two traveling therapists there. The other traveler was a physical therapist named Jen who had come from up-state New York. She had just broken up with her boyfriend of several years and had taken the job in Cedar Point to get away for a while. We instantly bonded and became good friends. I didn't know it initially, but as our time in Cedar Point progressed, Jen would be my savior - my refuge in the storm.

Pauline and I had a great time when I first got to Cedar Point. We quickly settled into a nice routine. We would have coffee and breakfast together and then I would head off to work. In the evenings I would make dinner for the two of us and we would spend time together. On the weekends, Pauline and I drove around, taking in the sights around her home town.

When Pauline had things to do, I would hang out with Jen. She and I had a great time exploring and hiking the local trails, or driving seventy miles to the closest mall to do some shopping.

The first few weeks flew by quickly and everything was going well. I had even accepted the fact that I was being introduced as Pauline's "friend" when we would run into her friends and family around town. I can't say that I enjoyed it, but I was honoring her privacy.

I had been in Cedar Point for about a month when I received a call from one of my best friends, Lori. She was going to be in Seattle for business and had made arrangements to spend the weekend with me in Cedar Point, which was fine with Pauline.

That weekend, one of the neighbors was having a BBQ and had invited the three of us to join them. So we did. I was very happy to have Lori with me as I did not know any of these people.

At one point during the BBQ, Pauline was talking with friends, and Lori and I were in another part of the neighbor's house getting some food. One of the neighbors came up to me and said, "So, you are here visiting your mother. How is that going?"

I just about dropped my plate. This was the first time anyone had confronted me about who I really was.

I'm sure Pauline had not said a word about it. I can only assume that this person had just figured it out since Pauline and I looked so much alike. I had to make a split second decision, and decided to be true to my word, so I responded, "It's going quite well, thank you." That was all I said and that was the end of the conversation.

My mistake came several days later. Pauline and I were driving home from dinner at one of her friend's house. I don't know why I did it, but I told her about the conversation I had had with one of the neighbors at the BBQ the weekend before. I think I was trying to give her a heads-up about the fact that people did know that I was her daughter. Pauline was silent.

When we got home, I went to the basement to change my clothes and wash my face. After that, I went upstairs to make a cup of tea before going to bed. I was standing in the kitchen when Pauline came out of her bathroom. She stood there with her hands on her hips, glared at me and started yelling.

I don't recall the exact words, but it went something like, "How dare you tell the neighbors that you are my daughter! You had no right to disregard my privacy like that! You have no idea what I have been through and how I feel! I can't believe you would do such a horrible thing!"

Anyone who knows me would tell you that I don't like confrontation. In a situation like that, I would typically just start crying and walk away. But now, for the first time in my life, I found my courage. I was angry and hurt and somehow found the words to reply.

"I have respected your privacy! I haven't gone around advertising the fact that I am your daughter. How do you think I feel when I am with you and you introduce me as your friend? I came here to spend time with you and I can't even be who I really am! I told you before I came here that if anyone asked me straight up about who I am, that I would not lie, and that is exactly what happened. I don't even know why I am here! Maybe I should just pack my things and leave!"

With tears streaming down my cheeks, I stormed past her and down the steps to the basement, slamming the door behind me. Thank God for my cats in that moment. They were always perceptive of my feelings and hurried to my side to comfort me.

I sat there sobbing. I didn't know what to do. I still had eight weeks of my speech therapy contract left. I couldn't just get in my car and drive back to Arizona. Maybe I could stay with Jen. All I knew was that I no longer wanted to be in that house with that woman!

About fifteen minutes later, Pauline came downstairs. She had calmed down and had thought about what I had said. She apologized for her outburst and asked if I would be willing to stay. She said that this was a growth process for both of us and we could work through it together, if I was willing. I decided to stay.

The next day was a Saturday and Pauline had errands to run. While she was gone I phoned my parents in Wisconsin. I immediately burst into tears and told them how grateful I was to have been adopted and to have been raised in such a loving home by such wonderful people. My dad said, "Well, we love you unconditionally and you will never have to hide the fact that you are our daughter." He always knew how to make me feel better.

I spent a lot of time with Jen over the next couple weeks. I was so grateful to have a friend to hang with when I felt like I had to get out of the house.

I also called my friend and coach, Phil. There were many emotions stirring inside of me and I didn't know how to handle them. Phil said that he would work with me and help me through the process. Again, he had me working with affirmations. Some of them were of forgiveness toward Pauline, and others were of self-love for myself.

The most difficult affirmation he had me write was, "I am perfect just the way I am." I was to write that affirmation and pay attention to what the "little voice in my head" had to say about it. Then I was to write another positive affirmation to negate the awful things that "little voice" was screaming back at me. The process took about thirty minutes every day because I was to write it out three times in the first person, three times in the second person and three times in the third person format. Each time that little voice had something to say: things like "If you're so perfect, why did your own mother give you away?" It took several weeks and a lot of tears before I could write that affirmation and actually believe it.

Phil also took me through a timeline exercise. It was a visualization process - a type of hypnosis to re-program my subconscious. This exercise would help me rewrite my script about how I felt coming into this world.

Under hypnosis, I was actually back in the womb and listening to Pauline as she told her parents that she was pregnant. I could hear them telling her that they would have to send her away for an abortion. Immediately, I felt hurt and full of anger at her parent's response. Phil brought me out of that hypnotic state and we talked about the feelings I had experienced.

I don't know exactly how Phil did it, but when he took me back to the womb the second time, I could see myself, propped up on one elbow and thinking, "Ha Ha! I don't care what you people think because I am coming into this world anyway, and you can't stop me!"

That exercise was extremely healing for me and helped me to understand just a little bit of what Pauline had gone through, too.

As my time in Cedar Point went on, Pauline and I did mend our relationship to a certain extent. We had some good times and some great laughs. She really did have a great sense of humor. My thirteen week assignment was to end in November, but I decided to extend my stay for another eight weeks since things were going fairly well.

For Thanksgiving, Pauline and I took a trip to Oregon to spend the holiday with her sister and brother-in-law, and for the first time, I had a chance to meet their daughter, my only biological cousin. It was a great time had by all and I felt like I was truly welcomed by the family.

Pauline and I were doing well. However, it wasn't all smooth sailing to the end of my time in Cedar Point. The side of Pauline that I had seen years ago when Paulette was visiting her in California was still there. It seemed like Pauline could always find something to criticize about each and every person with whom she came into contact. In hindsight, I believe that she found fault in others to make her feel better about herself.

It even happened to Jen. It was mid-December and Jen had invited Pauline and me over for dinner. She had spent all day cooking a wonderful meal. When we sat down at the table to eat, the first thing Pauline did was make a rude comment about the fact that the silverware was in the wrong place (per etiquette) at each setting.

I was appalled and embarrassed! I think she may have been trying to educate Jen in proper table setting, but it didn't come across that way. It's interesting how much of an impact one small comment can make. We had had a nice visit until that point in time. Even though Jen seemed to brush off the comment, I was acutely aware of the fact that it had been hurtful to her.

Living with that side of Pauline was challenging for me. I had spent years attempting to surround myself with happy, positive people. What I sensed from Pauline was a deep-seated pain and anger but I never had the courage to talk with her about it. Instead, when it was too much to handle, I would just spend more time with Jen.

My contract in Cedar Point ended the first week in January. The day before I was to leave and head back to Arizona, Pauline asked if I would go with her to see her uncle who lived just down the road. She and I had gone to dinner with him once a week while I was there and of course I had been introduced to him as Pauline's friend.

I didn't think anything of it, so I went along. To my surprise, as I was saying my goodbye, Pauline chimed in. She said to her uncle, "I have something to tell you." There was a pause. Pauline took a deep breath and continued, "Paula isn't just my friend. She is my daughter."

His response shocked both of us when he very casually said, "Yah, I know that."

That was a huge breakthrough for Pauline. She had been so ashamed and afraid, and now that burden had been lifted.

The next morning I was up, packed and ready to go before the sun came up. Just as I was about to leave Pauline gave me a big hug and thanked me for having stayed so long. She said she felt great and that my stay had been a wonderful healing process for both of us. I agreed, got in my car and headed home.

Chapter Eleven

I was happy to be back in Arizona. I had accepted another traveling assignment in Payson which is eighty miles north of Phoenix. The facility in which I was working set me up in one of their assisted living apartments and allowed me to have my cats with me. I would stay there Monday through Friday, then pack up the cats and head back to the valley to stay in my condo on the weekends.

I was feeling good about where I was in life, except for the fact that I was still alone. I thought about joining an online dating service but it didn't feel right. I still yearned for someone to share my life, but I also realized that I couldn't force the issue.

I remember very clearly the turning point. It was the evening of Thursday, February 9, 2006. I was in my assisted living apartment and decided to have a heart-to-heart with God. I said to God, "Lord, I know you are always there for me. You know that I would like to have a partner in life, but so far, that hasn't happened.

So, I am not going to worry about it anymore. I am going to give it up to you and trust that if my life plan includes a husband, you will send him to me when the timing is right." And with that, I let it go.

The next day was Friday. I finished work, packed up the cats and headed back to my condo for the weekend. When I got home, I took the cats and my luggage up to the condo and headed out again to do some shopping.

As I pulled into the parking lot of the first store, my phone rang. It was my friend Becky from California. She was very excited and said that she had met a man who would be perfect for me. She told me that over the holidays this man had accompanied a friend of her husband to their home. He seemed like a very nice gentleman and lived in Arizona. She had told him about me and he was open to meeting me. She asked if I was open to meeting him and I said yes, so she gave me his phone number. His name was Jim.

I ended the call with Becky and decided to give Jim a call. We had a nice conversation and decided to meet the next day, February 11, for our first date. God does work in mysterious ways!

Jim and I hit it off and started seeing each other when I was home on weekends. By the middle of April, my traveling assignment was over and I went back to work in Phoenix, which meant Jim and I could spend more time together. We were developing a wonderful relationship.

Life was good. I had a good career, was dating a great guy and was in a good place with my relationship with Pauline - or so I thought.

At this point in the story, I have to make a confession. I have always had a challenge with getting birthday gifts to people in a timely manner, whether it's friends or family. I almost always call on time, but the actual gift may not show up until a few weeks after the big day. It's a flaw that I am very much aware of, but haven't corrected. Most of my family and friends just see it as my M.O., and don't hold it against me.

Let's fast forward a couple months to the beginning of July. Jim and I had just finished an early morning hike when I said, "Remind me to buy and mail a gift to Pauline for her birthday. I told her I would send a gift and I haven't done so yet, and she is going to be mad."

Jim asked, "When was her birthday?"

I replied, "The end of May."

He asked, "Well, didn't you call her?"

"Yes," I replied, "but I told her I would send a gift and haven't yet."

Jim asked, "So what's the big deal? At least you called her on her birthday. That's the important part."

I said, "Well, you don't know Pauline. She's all about etiquette and I would imagine she is very upset by now so I really need to get something in the mail."

It was just three days later when I received what I can only describe as the most hurtful and hateful letter from Pauline. As I read the letter, it was as if she had taken a knife, stuck it right through my heart and twisted!

I don't recall the exact wording, but she wrote about how disappointed she was in me. In the letter she said that I was a person who could not be relied upon - that I was not a person of my word. She said that I had hurt her immensely by saying I would send a gift and hadn't done so. She went on to say that she had been thinking of my stay in Cedar Point and had come to the conclusion that I hadn't gone there to spend quality time with her or to find my father. Instead, she felt that the true reason I had gone to Cedar Point was to get back at her for something that had happened forty years ago, over which she had absolutely no control! She went on to say that she would never again depend on me for anything.

I read the letter a second time, in total disbelief. Where did that amount of anger come from? Surely, it could not have been spurred only by the fact that I hadn't sent a gift!

I know Pauline expected me to call. I know she thought I would come crawling back, begging for forgiveness.

I thought about that letter for a few days. When the time came, I did not call, but sent her an email. In that email I told her that I had received her letter. I went on to reiterate the fact that I had, indeed, gone to Cedar Point to spend time with her and to see Brad, not to hurt her. Then I ended the email by writing that if she truly believed that I was such an evil, vindictive person, then perhaps this relationship was no longer healthy for either one of us.

Her response came the next day, in an email, stating that she was appalled that I had sent an email instead of calling. She stated that it was extremely rude of me to send an email when she knew for a fact that I wasn't a person who liked to correspond in that fashion, but preferred to speak on the phone. Again, she was thoroughly disappointed!

That's it, I thought. This was not a person I wanted in my life anymore. I did not deserve to be treated that way. I understood that Pauline had her own pain, but that was no excuse. I still had the letter she sent. It was just too nasty and negative and was certainly not healthy. I had to get rid of that energy, so I decided to burn the letter.

Prior to destroying it, I told Jim about the letter and read it to him. He couldn't believe it either. The thing I loved about Jim was the fact that he always tried to see both sides and wanted to help. He tried to help me see that the letter was just a way for Pauline to vent her feelings. He thought I should just give it some time, think it over, try to see her point of view, and then maybe, eventually, I would want to call her to smooth over the situation. He said, "She is your mother. You are all that she has. You don't have to be close to her, but you may not want to totally cut her out of your life."

About a month later, I decided to call Pauline. She spent the first ten minutes of the call restating everything she had written in the letter. I just swallowed my pride and listened to her. The end result was that she felt she had to protect herself from more pain and disappointment. She said we could move forward, but that she would never again expect anything from me. I was fine with that.

I had gone through a lot of personal growth. Initially, I had thought that finding my biological mother would give me the answers to questions I had and that it would miraculously heal the void I had felt for so long. Now, I was at a point in my life where I realized that the void can only be filled when one comes to the place of self-acceptance and self-love. I had made it to that point. I no longer required approval or acceptance from others to know and believe that I was a good person. I loved myself.

Chapter Twelve

Jim and I continued to date and develop our relationship. I won't say it was complete bliss. Like any relationship, we had our growing pains.

Jim was a very private person and didn't like people knowing his business - even me, who he was dating! Often, when he had plans without me, he would just say that he was going out with friends, but wouldn't give any details. It made me crazy! He was also a person who liked to do whatever he wanted to do, when he wanted to do it, and he would not do things if he didn't think it would be fun.

For example, after we had dated for several months, I invited him to accompany me to Wisconsin for my grandmother's 90th birthday party, which was on the 4th of July. I really wanted him to go with me, but he declined.

We had several conversations about his being so aloof, and he would respond by telling me that he had shared more with me than with any other person he had ever dated, including his ex-wife. That didn't make me feel any better.

We had dated for about a year when I had reached my limit. I cared very deeply for Jim, but I couldn't take it anymore. I did not want to be in a relationship that was filled with secrecy. I called him one morning around 8 a.m. and asked if he was still at home. When he said that he was still home, I said, "Good, stay there because I am coming over." I was on my way to break up with him.

I arrived at Jim's house and I immediately sensed that he knew something was up. I sat down at his kitchen counter, looked him in the eye and said, "I have been thinking. I know that you are a very private person and that you don't like to share details with a lot of people. I also know that you are a person who wants to do what you want to do, and if it isn't fun, you won't do it. That's okay. I can't make you change that part of you, but if that is who you are, then I don't think you are the right person for me."

He instantly replied, "Look, you love me and I love you. We have invested a year into this relationship and I don't want to throw that away. I know there are things that I need to change. I just need to know if this is completely over or if there is a way we can work through it."

I looked at him and said, "I'm glad you know that there are things you need to change, but I don't really care about that. What I want to know is whether or not you WANT to change. There is a difference. It's like smoking. A person can know that they need to stop smoking, but until they WANT to stop smoking, nothing will happen."

He looked at me like a deer in headlights. There was silence for a long time while he processed what I had just said. Then, after some time, he said, "I want to change." With that, we continued to talk about our relationship and decided to give it another shot.

Ironically, that was the first time either of us had said the "L" word.

Our relationship progressed and within a couple months of that pivotal conversation we decided to take it to the next level. No, we did not get engaged. Instead, we decided to live together.

Remember the saying, "The older you get, the more you get set in your ways?" Well, it's true. Living with Jim was a huge adjustment for me. Oh, sure, I had lived with female roommates for sixteen years, in college and after, but that was very different from living as a couple with the man you love. Plus, for the past six years I had lived by myself. I had my own routine, my own way of doing things, my own schedule. I wasn't used to including another person in every decision I made, day in and day out.

Thank goodness Jim had been married before and he knew what to expect. He was very understanding and easy going as we figured out how to live together and mesh our two worlds into one. It took work and a great deal of compromise, but as time passed, we developed OUR routine.

Jim did eventually accompany me to Wisconsin. I believe it was a Christmas celebration at my parent's house when he had the chance to meet my entire family for the first time. After everyone was gathered, Jim looked at me and said, "You must be adopted. You are so short, compared to everyone else!"

It was like being in the land of the giants. My mom was 5'7" and my dad was 5'10". My brothers were both over 6 feet tall. My three nephews ranged from 6'2" to 6'8", and my two nieces were 5'10" and 6 feet tall. I was the runt of the litter, at 5'6". Again, I was reminded that I was different – that I didn't look like everyone else.

I told Jim that Pauline wasn't very tall either, but since he had not met her, he could only compare me to my family. Good thing he loved me just the way I was.

Every once in a while, in conversation, Jim would mention Pauline and ask how I was feeling about her. He knew I was harboring some pain and anger toward her and he was trying to help me work through it and let it go, but I wasn't ready. My relationship with Pauline had come to a point where we didn't communicate except to send birthday and Christmas cards to each other, and I was fine with that. So, Jim would let it go for a few months before bringing it up again.

I felt like I was in a really good place in my life. I had come to a point where I actually liked and loved myself, and I had attracted into my life the one thing I had wanted more than anything for so many years - a partner with whom to share my life. I thought I had it all, but as time went by, I started to get frustrated. Yes, I was living with the man I loved, but I wanted more. I wanted a deeper commitment. I wanted to be married.

There were times in the first year of living with Jim when I brought up the topic of a deeper commitment, but Jim was happy with our relationship just the way it was. I let it go for a while, but in my mind, I had a deadline. I had decided for myself that if we weren't at least engaged by the time we had lived together for two years, I was going to leave.

I had sacrificed so much to get to this point. I was forty-two years old and had given up the hope of ever having children. I wasn't going to just live with a man forever and give up the hope and dream of being married.

It was September 25, 2008 and Jim and I were eleven days into a two week trip to Egypt. We were on an island in the middle of the Nile River, touring the Temple of Philae, which is dedicated to Isis, the Goddess of Love. At the end of the tour our guide gave us some free time to do our own exploring.

Jim grabbed my hand and started pulling me down the hill away from the temple and toward the river bank, saying that he had something to show me. I had no idea what was going on. There happened to be a cement wall at the edge of the river and Jim had me stand on the wall with him next to me so one of the other gentlemen in our tour group could take a picture of us.

Just as the picture was about to be taken, Jim knelt down on one knee, took my hand and asked me to marry him! I was completely surprised! Jim popping the question was the last thing I expected at that moment. My mind was whirling, my knees buckled a little bit, and after several long seconds I said, "Yes."

Chapter Thirteen

Neither Jim nor I were in a rush to get married, although I think I wanted to do so more quickly than he. Somehow, the timing never seemed right. There was always something happening that would make us think we had to wait.

I was still working as a speech therapist, and Jim was working as a realtor. We were doing fine. Then the housing bubble burst in Arizona and the bottom fell out of the market, leaving Jim in a tough spot.

A year after our engagement, we ended up moving into a rental in Cave Creek, Arizona. We had signed a nine month lease while we looked for home to buy. Finally, in June, 2010, we purchased and moved into our home in Cave Creek. We had been engaged for a year and a half and still had made no plans for a wedding.

As time went by, my perception started to change. More than anything, I had always wanted to be married. Now, having been in a relationship with Jim for four years, having finally gotten to the place where someone actually loved me enough to ask me to marry them and having lived together for three years, I was content. I actually started to think that maybe we should just stay engaged for the rest of our lives. Why should we get married, anyway? It's not like we were planning on having children.

Maybe it was just fear of that final commitment, or possibly, I was trying to justify being engaged forever without being married. I started to think that if our relationship didn't work out, then it would be a lot easier to separate if we never had the legal bond of marriage. It was almost as if I was putting up a wall of numbness around me for protection.

It was a cool evening in the beginning of November, 2011. Jim and I were out at a local restaurant with our friend Donna. As we sat on the patio after dinner, the topic of marriage came up in conversation. Donna looked at Jim and me and said, "You two should just do it! You love each other. You've been engaged for more than three years already. What's the hold up? If you know you are committed to each other and that you want to spend the rest of your lives together, do it. Get married!" That was the night we made the decision. We would get married and solidify our commitment.

We immediately started to think about when and where we would get married. I had always dreamt of a traditional wedding, me in a white dress, walking down the aisle with my dad; my closest friends and family in attendance. I did not, however, have a set place in mind. I didn't have to be married in a specific church in

Wisconsin. As a matter of fact, I had lived outside of Wisconsin most of my adult life. My family was there, along with a few of my close friends, but Jim and I had family and friends all over the country. No matter where we got married, a majority of people would have to travel.

We decided to get married in Phoenix and set the date for March 3, 2012, when my parents would be in Arizona for their annual winter vacation. We had just four months to plan and prepare. It was a whirlwind of activity!

To keep it simple, I asked my friend Becky to be my matron of honor and Jim asked his son to be his best man. That was the extent of the wedding party. Instead of a white dress, I decided to wear ivory. The wedding color was ivory with just a splash of burgundy. We were to be married in the most beautiful Catholic Church in the area, something that was very important to Jim. We invited our closest family and friends - a list that could have been several hundred, but was narrowed down to eighty-five guests. Our cake was four layers, with three different flavors. I chose a bouquet of ivory roses with a few burgundy orchids. The reception was to be held in a beautiful building with huge glass windows overlooking a pond and the greens of a golf course. It would be simple and elegant.

The hardest decision I had to make was whether or not to invite Pauline to my wedding. We were still at the point where the only contact we had was to send birthday and Christmas cards to each other. Jim was very supportive and said that it was up to me and that he would honor any decision I made.

I knew that Pauline would have attended if asked, but the only thing I could imagine was that she would for sure find something that was not correct as far as etiquette goes. I didn't want to spend my wedding day worrying about what she might say.

I also felt that if I sent her an invitation, it would be out of guilt - feeling like I should invite her because she was my birth mother and not because I truly wanted her there. After some serious soul searching I decided that I wanted to fully enjoy my big day with my closest family and friends, so I did not invite Pauline to my wedding.

I don't think I slept much in the four months before the wedding. There was so much to do and so little time to do it. There were set-backs and miracles in the planning process, but eventually, it all worked out.

Finally, the day arrived. I was a nervous wreck! Thank God for Becky. She and I had a nice breakfast, including a glass of Champagne, to calm my nerves. My friend Ericka did our hair and makeup, and Becky and I set out for the church.

The florist and photographer were waiting for us. Becky, my mom and I were in a private room on one side of the church while Jim and his son were in a room on the other side. As Becky helped me into my dress a flood of emotion was flowing through me. I was excited, scared and nervous. I couldn't breathe. I had been waiting for this day for forty-five years! Finally, my greatest wish in life was about to come true.

The guests had arrived, the organist was playing beautiful music and the time had come. I walked to the entrance of the church, met my father and took his arm. I was about to cry, but thankfully, my father, with his sense of humor, had me laughing as we walked down the aisle. There I was, surrounded by family and friends, all here to celebrate this day with me. My father walked me to the front of the church, kissed my cheek, and gave my hand to Jim. Thirty minutes later, we were husband and wife.

The reception lasted till 8 p.m., but the party went on till midnight at the resort where we were all staying. As I lay in bed that night, nestled next to my husband, a sense of happiness and peace flowed through me.

This moment in time was the culmination of a life long journey: from being a child with low self-esteem and poor self-confidence, to the realization of abandonment issues, through the years of personal growth, and finally to a place of self-worth and self-love!

My identity no longer depended on where I had come from or on being Pauline's biological child or my parent's adopted daughter. It didn't depend on being Jim's wife either. That void inside of me no longer existed.

In the middle of the night I got up, went into the bathroom and looked in the mirror. It was then that I realized "I look like me." I love me, and that's enough.

Afterword

Writing this book has been a cathartic experience for me. Looking back on my journey, I am filled with gratitude for every step of the process.

I first contemplated writing my story twelve years ago, imagining a book that would be read by a multitude of adoptees who could relate to my struggles. I was only a few years into my own personal growth at that time. In retrospect, I realize that I did not start writing at that time because the story was still unfolding. *I Look Like Me* was not meant to be a book about struggle. Instead, it is a book of hope.

All individuals are faced with challenges in life which can hold us back and even break us down if we let them. The beauty is that those challenges can also be seen as an opportunity for growth. The key is awareness.

Once we are aware, there are many ways to work through and release ourselves from the struggle. As mentioned in my story, I was able to utilize several methods in my journey to self-love.

I encourage anyone dealing with the challenges of abandonment, low self-esteem/self-worth, or just not feeling good about who you are to explore and utilize methods which will work for you. You might try hiring a life coach, hypnotherapy, utilizing positive affirmations, attending personal growth seminars and/or reading self-help books.

Those years of intense personal growth were a turning point in my life. Does that mean that I am at the end of my journey? Absolutely not! The journey never ends. There is always room for growth and there will always be times and events that bring back those feelings of abandonment.

The true blessing, however, is the fact that once we reach a place of self-love, we are better equipped to handle those times of uncertainty. Events and circumstance which initially would have sent us into a tailspin for months or even years, are quickly identified and acknowledged, allowing us to release them.

By reaching a place of self-love, we can realize that we are perfect souls worthy of all life has to offer. In addition, the opportunity for true forgiveness presents itself. We can forgive ourselves for the years of self-abuse, as well as forgive others that we may have blamed as the cause of our issues. I believe that we are all perfect souls having a human experience and I also believe that everyone is doing the best they can at all times.

Each of us has a beautiful light inside, with talents and gifts which only we can offer. When we recognize that truth and begin to appreciate and embrace our uniqueness, we can begin to see our true value. To experience self-love is the key to true happiness. Once you have it, your entire being will light up. I encourage you to find your light and let it shine!

Sharing Some Of
My Favorite Books

Infinite Possibilities: The Art of Living Your Dreams by Mike Dooley

You Can Heal Your Life by Louise Hay

Radical Forgiveness by Colin Tipping

Excuse Me, Your Life Is Waiting by Lynn Grabhorn

The Four Agreements by Don Miguel Ruiz

The Game of Life and How to Play It by Florence Scovel Shinn

Awaken the Giant Within by Antony Robbins

The Five Love Languages by Gary Chapman

The Gifts of Imperfection by Brene' Brown

These are some of the books that helped me with my healing process.

Some Final Thoughts About The Role Of Animals In Our Lives

Animals are true blessings in our lives. They provide an enormous amount of unconditional love and comfort.

I feel compelled to pay tribute to my cats Madison and Dusty. It recently occurred to me that they came into my life just as I was starting my personal awakening and journey to self-love. They were there by my side every step of the way.

There were times when I was down and out and felt like ending it all, but I couldn't do it because I had to take care of my girls. In retrospect, I wasn't taking care of them; they were taking care of me. They gave me purpose when all else seemed hopeless.

As I mentioned in the main story, Dusty lived an additional seven years after her bout with cancer. She went to kitty heaven on December 30, 2009. She was with me for eleven years.

Madison was with me for fifteen years. She was my constant companion. Somehow, I feel that the writing of this book was a turning point for me - closure in many ways - and Madison saw me through the entire process. She was there, sitting by my side every morning as I sat on the patio writing my story. She went to kitty heaven on March 28, 2014.

I am truly grateful to have had them in my life and they will be with me in spirit forever.

About The Author

Paula K. Dieck is an author, certified life coach, certified trainer for Infinite Possibilities and Reiki Master-Teacher. She received a Bachelor of Science Degree in Education in 1988 and a Master of Science Degree in Communicative Disorders in 1990. Paula had a successful 23 year career in Speech-Language Pathology.

In 2000, Paula attended her first personal growth seminar which changed her life and helper her realize her true passion.

Today, through coaching, Infinite Possibilities classes and her weekly email, "Pearls for Positive Change," Paula uses her skills to assist others in discovering their own self-worth and in coming to a place of complete self-love.

To learn more about Paula or to schedule individual coaching please visit: www.ilooklikeme.com or contact her at paula@ilooklikeme.com

Made in the USA
San Bernardino, CA
11 October 2014